Dedication

I was able to write so much about celebration
thanks to the following important occasions:

The birth day of my mom, Elsie, which later became my birth day
The birth days of my siblings: Art Jr., Terry Sr., Laurie, Bill, and Scott
The birth days of my children: Frank, Cathy, and Deena
The birth days of my grandchildren: Jasmine, Mackenzie, and Aysia
The many special events created by my dearest friends Kelly and Gill

Acknowledgments

My writing was encouraged and supported by

Expert "read and fix" lovingly provided by Kelly Ryan
Friendship from Judith Anne, Roni, Maxine, Misty, Dan, Harvey, and Evelyn
Lively conversations with a patient and perceptive Bruce Lansky
TLC given me and my work by Liya at Meadowbrook
Phone and e-mail encouragement from Minneapolis, St. Paul,
Indianapolis, Long Island, Boston, Denver, Chicago, and Jacksonville
Unconditional help given by the family "Self-Help King" T.J.

TABLE OF CONTENTS

PART THREE: PARTY THEMES

PART FOUR:
PARTY TACTICS

PART FIVE:
PARTY-PLANNING
HELPERS

INTRODUCTION

How to Use This Book

Celebration is a vitally important part of our lives. During those happy times shared with family, friends, neighbors, and coworkers we grow personally and improve our relationships.

Whenever you show appreciation for others by celebrating with them, one-on-one or in a group, you, too, benefit from the effort. I am sure you can remember the feelings of excitement, cheerfulness, affection, and pride you experienced when you took part in a festive occasion.

Pick a Party contains ideas, suggestions, and tips to help you easily and afford-ably create successful and memorable celebrations for every life cycle occasion, holiday, and special event. You will find traditional and familiar party ideas, as well as innovative, unusual options—for you to pick and choose and mix and match.

In addition to over 140 parties, *Pick a Party* also provides everything you may need when planning your party. The Party Tactics chapter will guide you through planning surprise, potluck, come-as-you-are, outdoor, and other popular events, and the Party-Planning Helpers chapter will remove the "where" and "how" frustra-tions inherent in party planning.

Finally, the pièce de résistance—the feature of *Pick a Party* that you will love—the Theme Grid. With the aid of this tool, you can match your occasion or holiday to a number of theme options to select a theme that fits your needs. For example, you may discover that a Bridal Shower party is cross-referenced with the Victorian, Twenties, or Hawaii theme. You can then read the instructions for those themes and choose the one you think will best compliment your celebration. The grid will save you time and frustration, and enable you to choose among themes you may not have even thought to consider.

Hooray! Now that you own *Pick a Party,* you can say a final good-bye to your party-planning anxiety. As a host, guest, or committee member, you can follow the ideas presented in this book precisely, or use them to inspire you to design your own perfect party. Hopefully, you will enjoy party planning so much, you will use any excuse to plan a celebration.

Remember, no matter the size of the celebration, be sure to follow the *Pick a Party* rule: You as the host or hostess should always have as much fun, or more, than your guests.

Part One
LiFE CYCLE OCCASIONS

A lifetime is filled with many marvelous reasons to celebrate—from its beginning to its end. A happy occasion, such as a birthday, a wedding, a birth, a graduation, or an anniversary, deserves, and usually gets, a festive celebration. In addition, our lives are filled with many smaller milestones—each one worthy of commemoration of some kind.

This section lists every significant life cycle occasion, and touches upon the traditions and current trends followed in observing each one. For the more adventurous, each party also has a "twists" section with innovative party-planning suggestions. You can use the information in this section to follow the traditional path while planning your party, arrange for a few surprises along that familiar path, or stray off the traditional path for a whole new party destination.

Whether you're planning a small, intimate gathering, or a large, blow-out bash, be sure to add a generous amount of humor and to personalize many facets of the party plan with the name(s) of the guest(s) of honor, for a memorable and meaningful celebration.

As family and friends gather to celebrate life cycle occasions, they renew and strengthen relationships by showing each other appreciation and admiration. That is why celebration is a major contributing factor to good emotional health and well-being. Isn't it good to know that whenever you host a party, you not only add to your guests' happiness but you also improve their health?

BIRTHDAY: FIRST

This party is really a Birth Day festivity that provides the baby's friends and relatives the opportunity to socialize in a casual and whimsical way. Since your guests' ages will most likely vary greatly, you will have to keep the party plans generic.

Trends
- In the past, first birthday parties tended to be small, uncomplicated gatherings of family and friends, including children of all ages; the baby messed up the cake for a photo opportunity, while Mom, Dad, or older siblings opened gifts.
- Now, families tend to celebrate baby's first birthday with an elaborate "coming out" party, complete with professionally printed invitations, gala decorations, party favors, and even hired entertainment. After all, baby's arrival was very important, so baby's family is ready to throw a real welcome bash.

Tips
- Have brightly wrapped gifts for all the children who attend the party, as well as little mementos for the grownups.
- Take instant photos of each guest or family member with the baby; these photos make festive party favors.
- Don't spend a fortune on a costumed character for this party. Any willing adult can put on a rented or improvised costume for just as much fun.
- Prepare the baby for the party with a long nap that ends just as the party begins.
- Videotape the party activities. Nothing delights children more than watching movies of themselves as children, especially if the movies include Mom, Dad, and siblings acting silly, like little children.
- Videotape self-introductions of each guest with wishes for the baby and his or her parents.
- Be aware that clowns or other costumed characters may scare little children; be sure the entertainer is not too loud and doesn't come on too strong.

Twists
- Structure the party around the Kindergarten theme. (See page 93.) This delightful theme simulates an old-fashioned kids' birthday party with simple parlor games, festive decorations, and light refreshments. Adults join the children in all activities to compete for awards and prizes.

For other themes appropriate for your occasion, see the theme grid on page 188.

BIRTHDAY: KID'S

The biggest challenge party planners face is amusing and entertaining a pack of kids—for more than ten minutes. For one- to four-year-old kids, simply having other kids around creates a party. But when planning a party for a kid who is between five and twelve years old, you have to get out the Party Dictionary and call the Party Police!

Trends
- A theme is essential, whether it follows the current Disney rage or a Saturday morning cartoon. The party stores are filled with complete party supplies for the most popular themes, and most kids between the ages of four and eight will beg for one of them. While going this rout may be a little more expensive, such a party will please the child and actually save you time.
- Children between the ages of nine and twelve tend to want a less "childish" theme. They prefer such themes as Pirate's Party, Mystery Solving Party, Treasure Hunt, Beauty Spa Visit, Costume Party, Crafting Party, or a family outing.

Tips
- Make a big deal out of selecting, creating, addressing, and sending party invitations. For the birthday kid, the party starts with the invitations.
- Involve the whole family in party planning and preparation—a birthday is a family celebration. Younger children will feel less left out if they can help. Give them easy but useful tasks, such as putting stamps on the invitations or setting the table. (See Resources, #55, for activities and recipes.)
- Make sure that the birthday child is the first to open and enjoy the birthday presents. After presents have been opened, put them out of reach so they won't get lost or damaged. In the chaos of gift opening, try to keep track of who gave what. Keep a roll of tape on hand, and tape the cards to the gifts.

Twists
- Take an instant photo of the birthday kid holding up or wearing each gift. After the party, send the photo along with a thank-you note. This is especially nice for the people who sent a gift but couldn't attend the party.
- Enlist the help of high-school-aged kids to help during the party. Dress them up in costume, give them a crash course in face-painting and balloon-sculpting, get them to perform musical or drama shows, and finally, have them help you clean up. The young party guests will love having the older kids at the party, and you'll save a bunch of money.

For other themes appropriate for your occasion, see the theme grid on page 188.

BAR/BAT MITZVAH

The "coming of age" of a Jewish boy or girl—thirteenth birthday for a boy, and twelfth birthday for a girl—calls for a celebration that includes religious ceremonies as well as social gatherings. Family members and friends gather to honor the Bar/Bat Mitzvah child and to share feelings of pride, love, and spirituality. Whether your party calls for formal, black-tie wear or funky blue jeans, your guests are sure to have a memorable time if you have fun planning a happy and lighthearted event.

Trends
- The Bar/Bat Mitzvah weekend includes a Friday night and Saturday morning service at which the Bar/Bat Mitzvah recites an excerpt from the Torah (the Hebrew Bible) in front of friends, family, and congregation.
- The celebration sometimes also includes a special luncheon and/or a Saturday evening dinner/dance/party.
- The entire weekend, with the exception of the religious ceremonies, is often planned around a theme that represents one of the child's hobbies, talents, or interests, including the decor, entertainment, food, gifts, and favors.

Tips
- Finish the weekend with a casual Sunday brunch, which provides a chance for all guests to say their last farewells.
- Rent a van and hire a driver for the weekend to transport guests from and to the airport, and to and from the temple and party.
- If stumped for a theme, something as simple as a color scheme, the seasons (winter wonders, summer sunshine, fall fantasy, or spring song), or a catch phrase (such as "What a Gem!," which involves incorporating jewels, sparkle, and glitter into the party decor) can provide the basis for a super event.
- Once you choose a theme, brainstorm with creative friends or family members to generate dozens of theme-related ideas.
- Be sure to give party favors to all the children, matching gift to child's age.
- Arrange to have a welcome gift placed in each guest's hotel room. Use easy-to-pack-and-take-home containers and, preferably, nonperishable snacks.

Twists
- Plan a sensational on-the-move event on a boat, bus, train, or wagon.
- Have a bar/bat mitzvah party that involves favorite family activities, such as bowling, skating, horseback riding, or even cooking, especially if it is a "planned-for-kids" event.
- Consider planning a semiformal gala. You *can* keep the children occupied at such an event. Just be sure to plan fun activities: face painting, caricature drawing, computer generating of photos and photo buttons, karaoke singing, and dance instructing are activities that kids and adults can enjoy. Provide appropriate space, material, and instructions for each activity.

For other themes appropriate for your occasion, see the theme grid on page 188.

QUINCEANERA

(keen-se-an-yeah-ra)

Quince means fifteen in Spanish. Quinceanera is the Latino celebration of a girl's fifteenth birthday. This event celebrates the girl's debut into society as a young woman. The Quinceanera is equal in importance to a Bat Mitzvah (a coming-of-age for Jewish girls) or a wedding. Families from all income levels prepare a meaningful and festive celebration to present their daughters to society.

Trends

- The average Quinceanera celebration takes place in a hotel ballroom, country club, or banquet hall. The invitations are formal; the decorations, elaborate; and the food and beverages, lavish. Guests listen and dance to traditional Latino music and to any other popular entertainment.
- The girl of honor has attendants, who are selected much like bridesmaids, and an official escort, who is her companion for the entire event.
- Women dress in formal ball gowns, and men wear tuxedos.

Tips

- Economize by planning the event in your yard. Rent or borrow tents, tables, chairs, dance floors, lighting, and other props. Keep in mind, however, that unless you can borrow (from a church or a club) or cheaply rent all the necessary items, you may spend as much on a backyard event as you would have on an event held in an indoor space—where you wouldn't have to worry about weather conditions and about coordinating the set up and cleanup.

Twists

- Have a cooperative celebration to reduce the budget. Have relatives and friends supply the invitations, decorations, entertainment, food, and beverages. If you carefully coordinate all the people involved, to make sure that the celebration goes off without confusion and that nothing is lacking, the event can still be very elaborate and elegant, and will cut the cost tremendously.

For other themes appropriate for your occasion, see the theme grid on page 188.

BIRTHDAY: TEENS

Birthdays are just one occasion for teen parties. Other occasions include a teen or a Sweet 16 celebration, a prom or school dance, a team victory, or a "spontaneous congratulation" for a personal win. Keep in mind, however, that planning parties for teenagers involves a special set of challenges. Because today's young people are exposed to so many worldly and exciting things through movies, videos, and television, getting and keeping their attention takes ingenuity and dedication.

Trends
- Parties for this age group must have enough activities to keep the kids constantly absorbed. (Easy for me to say!) Dozens of books filled with games and activities are available to help you accomplish this impossible task.
- Expensive entertainment or equipment will not automatically make the party better or more interesting. A schedule of lively games, activities, and prize awards will generate as much excitement and pleasure, if not more.
- Food won't keep the kids busy for more than five or ten minutes. If they stay seated for longer than that, they have probably figured out a way to play with their food. So, set out a ton of "help-yourself" snack foods at food stations around the party room, and reserve seating for dessert only.
- On-the-go parties at fun centers are popular. Keep in mind, though, that it is hard to incorporate meaningful or traditional activities into such chaotic situations.

Tips
- Choose a party theme that all guests will like, not only the birthday child.
- Remember that although teens are sometimes very competitive, they are not always good sports—and they have fragile feelings and egos. Avoid prize drawings in which there are more losers than winners. Instead, award fancy medals to winners, and present all guests with favors/gifts that are equal in value.
- Do your children a big favor—teach them the art of being a good host and guest. For example, teach them to write thank-you notes—not only to acknowledge gifts received but also to thank hosts for parties attended.

Twists
- Plan a party around a do-it-yourself theme. Although such parties are quite messy, they are good for teens. Some ideas are Pizza Making, Cake or Cookie Baking, Arts & Crafts, and Makeovers.
- Have an outdoor party at a carnival or a street fair. Such parties are great because several things are going on at the same time, which cuts down on waiting time. Kids of all ages are not at their best when standing in line for too long.
- Organize an overnight party with a theme—teens love these.
  —*Great for Girls:* Hair and Makeup, Danceathon, Island Getaway, Fashion Fling, Bake and Take, Craftathon, MTV Madness, Clothing Exchange.
  —*Best Bets for Boys:* Tool Time/Woodworking, Sportsathon, Electronic Games.
  —*Unisex Themes:* Camping, Skating, Treasure Hunts, Board Games, Karaoke, Mystery, TV, and Movies.

For other themes appropriate for your occasion, see the theme grid on page 188.

BIRTHDAY: TWENTY-FIRST

Traditionally, turning twenty-one means bidding farewell to carefree youth. Most often, though, the most dramatic change in the guest-of-honor's life is that he or she can proudly show a valid ID card when out on the town. Legal celebrating is a great reason to celebrate!

Trends

- Twenty-first birthday parties have a built-in "drinking problem"—although the guest of honor is now of legal drinking age, the same may not be true of many of the guests, thus creating a touchy situation. Parents who organize the party can solve this problem by planning a bowling, skating, hayride, or arcade activity, with no drinking allowed, followed by a closely supervised sleep-over party that may include moderate drinking, but would preclude any drinking and driving.

Tips

- Show photos, slides, or videos of the guest of honor acting in ways that are now embarrassing, and call it a "farewell tribute to youth." You may find it necessary to collect photos from the guest-of-honor's friends and other relatives.
- Organize a rowdy and rollicking roast: Let guests tell their favorite guest-of-honor stories.

Twists

- Have a "21 at 21" party. Replicate the elegant atmosphere of the famous New York restaurant. Plan a semiformal, swanky affair—with favorite foods, blackjack, and sophisticated music—to salute the newly-turned-adult guest of honor.
- Design your celebration around a Twenties theme—an era when drinking was illegal for everyone. (See Roaring Twenties party, page 106.)
- Ask all the guests to come dressed as their parents—this party starter works well when all the guests are familiar with the people being imitated. Give a prize for the best performance.

BIRTHDAY: THIRTIETH

Some people think they are over-the-hill at thirty. Well, thirty is more like being over the mound, still approaching the hill. Now that folks are living to the age of 100, they don't get to the "hill" until they are sixty years old. So those turning thirty are only halfway up the big climb. However, they deserve a party anyway.

Trends
- Guests are often required to bring "how-to-stay-young" gifts, such as books and magazines on the topic, creams, vitamins, framed advertisements, related gizmos, and so on. Opening the gifts becomes a hilarious party activity.
- Over-the-Hill parties are rampant, so decor and party goods are readily available at party stores.

Tips
- Structure the party around a theme that follows the guest-of-honor's high-school days.
- Organize silly and/or sentimental roasts and "life story" presentations.
- Videotape all party activities and guest interviews.
- Procure posters and photo blowups of the cast of the television show *Thirty Something*. (See Resources, #10.)
- Decorate the party room with posters, advertisements, and equipment for "youth preservation."

Twists
- Suggest that guests choose gifts according to one of the following criteria:
  —in quantities of thirty (thirty pencils, cards, and so on).
  —at the cost of thirty pennies (30¢), nickels ($1.50), dimes ($3.00), or quarters ($7.50).
- Instruct the guests to dress as their version of how the guest of honor will look at age fifty or sixty; award prizes for the most creative costumes.
- Throw a Suddenly Suspicious party based on the belief that "you can't trust anyone over thirty":
  —Glue a piece of Mylar paper onto each invitation to represent a rearview mirror, and write the party details using such words and phrases as "never trust," "suspicious," "leery," "don't turn your back," "keep both eyes open," and so on.
  —Have the guests dress as detectives or super sleuths, and tell them to behave like jittery paranoids.
  —Post an official food taster at the buffet table.
  —Decorate the party room with signs that advertise security systems and private detectives, and rig the bathroom door with dozens of fake locks and latches.

For other themes appropriate for your occasion, see the theme grid on page 188.

BIRTHDAY: FORTIETH

Though no longer strictly considered to be the passage into middle age, hitting the big Four-O still summons up visions of going over-the-hill.

Trends
- Many people take the party on the road—to a bowling alley, ranch, skating rink, or pizza parlor. Such a party seems to fit this age group's casual lifestyle.
- Family-oriented outings, such as picnics, barbecues, or pool parties, are popular because the guest of honor and many of the guests usually have teenage children.
- Surprise parties seem to be the most popular host's choice for this celebration. Producing a surprise party can be a stimulating challenge that will most likely result in a memorable event. (See Party Tactics, page 156.)
- Costume parties are also very popular, for both adults-only and family events.

Tips
- Create a Time Capsule gift for the guest of honor. Include the daily paper; videotape of a television news show; a current photo of the guest of honor with family; memorabilia from a current job, such as a business card and letter-head; and a favorite piece of clothing. In years to come, this capsule will be a valued memento.
- If planning an adults-only event for your husband or wife, enlist the help of your children to prepare for the party and to greet guests. Once the party is rolling along, the children can make a graceful exit.

Twists
- Add a personal touch to the celebration by planning the party around the guest-of-honor's occupation, hobby or interest, favorite sport, favorite ethnic food, a "never-misses-it" television show, or the year of his or her high-school graduation. Play the music, serve the food, and have guests wear the clothing appropriate for one of the above theme options, and you have all the makings of a well-planned and extremely successful party. (See Resources, #40, 58.)
- Have a forties, wartime, big band event, costumes and all. (See Forties party, page 107.) Create some friendly competition with a forties trivia contest or a name-that-big-band-tune contest.

For other themes appropriate for your occasion, see the theme grid on page 188.

BIRTHDAY: FIFTIETH

This is a real biggy, as birthday bashes go. The guest of honor is in the prime of his or her life, when there is no such thing as too much fun. Regardless of personality traits or lifestyles, most half-centurions are ready to party hearty. Themes are almost imperative when planning this birthday party.

Trends
- Successful fiftieth birthday parties tend to center around the guest-of-honor's hobbies/pastimes, skills/talents, occupation, ethnic background, or personality traits.
- A party that features music, food, decor, and clothing from the guest-of-honor's high-school days is usually a huge success, and it can make a fifty feel like fifteen again.
- Fiftieth birthday parties seem to "want to be" planned as surprises.

Tips
- Consider reducing the amount of anxiety inherent in planning a surprise party by letting the guest of honor know that something will take place on a specific day, but leave the what, who, where, and how as a complete surprise. However, if you still want to plan a total surprise, see the Surprise tactic, page 156.

Twists
See the following popular themes for fiftieth birthday parties:
- Fabulous Fifties: A rock and roll revival starring characters from the television show *Happy Days*, with music reminiscent of *Dick Clark's American Bandstand*. (See Fifties party, page 108.) Guys gear up in leather jackets and blue jeans, and gals swirl and twirl in poodle skirts and cardigan sweater sets.
- This Is Your Life: A parody on the classic TV show, filled with humor and sentiment, with a gala party finale of food and drink, dancing, and reminiscing. (See This Is Your Life party, page 101.)
- Tribute to Elvis Presley and Marilyn Monroe: A party theme in which all guests come dressed as one of the movie idols. Expect a riotous party at which outgoing guests mix and mismatch the genders while portraying their favorites.
- You Must've Been a Beautiful Baby: A back-to-childhood theme, in which guests come over in their best diapers and Doctor Dentons to play with the guest of honor, drink from baby bottles, play baby games, and shake their pink or blue "booties."
- You Oughtta Be in Pictures: A nostalgia theme featuring movies popular during the past fifty years. Guests dress as entertainment stars for an evening of star gazing and reminiscing.
- Extra! Extra! Read All about 'Em!: A party planned around the newspaper/reporter theme. Guests dress to represent a major headline from the past fifty years.

For other themes appropriate for your occasion, see the theme grid on page 188.

BIRTHDAY: SIXTIETH

Considering today's medical technology, sixty may now be appropriately termed over-the-hill, which is not at all negative, since it suggests there may be sixty more on the trip down. However, since turning sixty may not be thrilling for the guest of honor, this party must be lighthearted and upbeat.

Trends
- Hosts frequently use the guest-of-honor's hobbies, interests, talents, and skills to set a theme, saving the occupation theme for a retirement party that may be right around the corner.
- Another theme possibility is the guest-of-honor's goal or dream, such as traveling, writing, building, developing inventions, or carrying out business schemes.
- Family parties are common, with guests' ages ranging widely—from grandchildren to grandparents.

Tips
- Choose gifts that will enhance leisure time: books, videos, tapes, and how-to materials.
- Play up the guest-of-honor's quirks, habits, or idiosyncrasies for a clever party motif. (One hostess made an incredibly successful party out of the fact that her husband's mania was to clean up long before a party's end. She sent the invitations in small bags, instructed guests to dress in trash bags, and used trash and garbage bags in the decorations. The finale was when all of the guests left the party room, returned with trash bags, and started policing the party area—two hours before the end of the party.)

Twists
- Have a preretirement spoof by asking guests to imitate the guest-of-honor's leisure time attire. This is especially amusing when adults and children participate.
- Choose a sixties theme for this occasion, complete with flowers, peace signs, and hippy paraphernalia. (See Sixties party, page 109.) Include a sixties sing-along for lively, interactive entertainment. Songs made famous by the Beatles, The Mamas and the Papas, and other sixties super stars will get your guests to "Sing a Song."

BIRTHDAY: SEVENTY-FIFTH

Now that the guest of honor has accumulated hoards of wisdom and insight, seventy-five can be a very delightful age. Friends, family members, and former workmates will show up in numbers to congratulate the guest of honor on reaching this milestone.

Trends
- Whether completely or partially retired, the guest of honor will enjoy any spirited, lively, and surprise-filled festivities.
- For someone who has not worked in ten to fifteen years, life probably revolves around leisure activities, hobbies, travel, and enjoying family, all of which make good party themes.
- If, however, the guest of honor is still working, a party theme that reflects the guest-of-honor's industry is quite appropriate.
- New work ventures make excellent party themes. People in this postretirement age group are constantly surprising those around them with their entrepreneurial projects and activities.

Tips
- Design a party to pay tribute to a late-in-life career start, including a home-business venture such as cake-decorating, or even a part-time job in a fast-food restaurant.
- Suggest that guests pool funds for one substantial gift, rather than having each guest give a small gift. Keep in mind that a person of seventy-five is usually trying to get rid of "stuff," not collect more.
- Give gift certificates for lessons, classes, seminars, and workshops, as well as for the corresponding equipment or materials.
- Remember that the gift of your time is always the best gift. Please the guest of honor with personal-time certificates for trips to the zoo, art gallery, movies, mall, or local casino. Or give personal-time certificates for quiet visits for tea or dinner.

Twists
- Plan a This Is Your Life tribute. Gather written, audio, or video messages, or even recorded telephone messages, and play/show them as party entertainment. (You can find inexpensive telephone recording devices at your local electronics store.) This is a great way to include guests who cannot attend the celebration. (See This Is Your Life party, page 101.)

For other themes appropriate for your occasion, see the theme grid on page 188.

BIRTHDAY: HUNDREDTH

Not long ago, the president of the United States sent four or five greetings each year to persons reaching the one-century mark. Today, it is not uncommon for him to greet five persons a month on their hundredth birthday. (See Resources, #32.) The reasons for this longevity vary from drinking a shot of whiskey every day to living in the mountain air. *I* think the guest of honor stays around because he or she doesn't want to miss his or her birthday party.

Trends
- The best way to accommodate the guest-of-honor's large accumulation of friends and family is to plan an open house that extends over several hours, rather than having a large group of people crowd in the party room for a short time.

Tips
- Stagger the hours of the party so that groups can gather at varying times, with slight overlap. For example: church members 1-3 P.M., neighbors and friends 3-6 P.M., and so on, with close relatives and friends attending the entire time. This is especially convenient if you are limited for space.
- Schedule special entertainment, such as a song or poem presentation, more than once during the party to accommodate multiple audience and to give the guest of honor a chance to absorb it thoroughly.
- Show photos, slides, movies, and videos in a designated area throughout the length of the party. Run a carousel slide show on a large screen to provide entertainment as well as decor.
- Keep music quiet, so it won't distract from the guest-of-honor's conversations. Popular music from the past eighty years will help spark memories.
- Occupy children by setting up a small activity table or play area. Decorate the children's area especially for the wee guests, and serve miniportions of food and beverages in special containers. You can also keep the children busy with small tasks, such as greeting the guests or bussing used paper cups and plates.

Twists
- Have young people read aloud messages from guests to the guest of honor.
- Choose gifts carefully. Giving a gift to someone who has lived a hundred years is a challenge. The finest gift is of one's time—a personal-time certificate for a special visit, errand, service, or, if possible, an outing. Anything from giving a manicure to addressing greeting cards to walking around the block with the centurion will add great pleasure to the guest-of-honor's life.
- Videotape a spoken greeting from each guest. Ask those who cannot attend to send photos and messages to be added to the tape.

For other themes appropriate for your occasion, see the theme grid on page 188.   **13**

ENGAGEMENT/ REHEARSAL DINNER

These festive occasions should be planned with the prospective newlyweds' interests, talents, personalities, and occupations firmly in mind. A personalized theme will enhance the party immensely, and, as with any theme, make party planning much easier.

Trends
- Since the guests at both parties tend to be people who may not know each other, the focus of the party should be the couple—something that all the guests have in common. A light, almost humorous, party atmosphere will put people at ease.

Tips
- Make sure to plan an engagement party that the engagement couple will like— avoid planning an engagement party that will make only you feel comfortable. For example: Don't entertain at the posh country club if the guests of honor would prefer the cozy and comfortable local pasta place.
- Use your judgment when planning the rehearsal dinner. This event can be more formal, since most guests will have met each other at least once; the anxiety of sprucing up and remembering which fork to use will not be increased by meeting strangers.
- Be sure to plan a comfortable way to introduce all guests to each other. The following is an easy and delightful way to do this: Pair each guest with another guest who is essentially a stranger. Have them swap personal information; then have each guest introduce their partner to the rest of the guests. This is a funny, lively, and spontaneous way to break the ice.

Twists
- Discover how the couple met. Sometimes the place and way that the couple met provides a perfect theme. Whether they first saw each other at a bowling alley, horse ranch, supermarket, or school, try to recreate the atmosphere with a special menu, a few props, and appropriate party decor. If possible, plan the event at the actual site, or a site that replicates the original.
- Create ample opportunity for guests to express sentimental thoughts. Make sure to have the necessary equipment (such as a video camera if you plan to tape messages to the couple) and sufficient time for these special moments. Inform all guests of this activity, so they can jot down a few words to say themselves, or to give to someone else to read aloud. These opportunities to share sentiments, joy, and even sadness are often the most important part of any personal event. Unfortunately, lack of planning often does not allow enough time for these personal moments.

For other themes appropriate for your occasion, see the theme grid on page 188.

WEDDING SHOWER

Every bride looks forward to her friends and relatives showering her with gifts and good-luck wishes before the wedding. The themes used to produce wedding showers are widely varied and quite entertaining—imagination seems to be the only limit.

Trends

- No-host showers—that is, where each guest pays for him- or herself at a nice restaurant or country club—are quite popular. The gift is usually significant and expensive, given cooperatively by the group. The shower organizers usually provide the invitations, favors, entertainment, and gift selection.
- Couples register for gifts at all imaginable stores, such as those selling computers, books, do-it-yourself supplies, sports equipment, office supplies, gourmet/gadgets, pet supplies, and trendy furniture. Finding shower gifts is a breeze with all of these resources.

Tips

- Throw a shower to help a busy, busy bride complete one of her wedding projects, such as making favors or decorations. Add delicious refreshments and the showering of gifts, and you'll have a party that will be innovative and a real lifesaver for the bride.
- Plan an absentee shower for the bride who lives miles away. Gather a group of friends or relatives who want to celebrate the happy occasion, and videotape all the festivities, including opening the gifts. Then send the party tape and the gifts to the bride. (See Resources, #43, 58, for more ideas.)

Twists

Consider the following popular themes for bridal showers:

- Room of the House: Guests bring gifts to be used in a designated room of the bride's home. Hosts send out invitations that provide such information as the color scheme, furnishing style, and special suggestions.
- Let's Get Organized: Guests choose gifts designed to help the bride get and stay organized in every room of the house, as well as in her life. Planner books and file and storage boxes make good gifts for this shower, and they are available in just about every color and motif imaginable.
- Many Meals Together: Guests bring gifts to help the couple celebrate special mealtimes, such as breakfasts, brunches, picnics, cocktails, dinners, and desserts.

For other themes appropriate for your occasion, see the theme grid on page 188.

COUPLE'S WEDDING SHOWER

The best coed wedding shower themes are whimsical, humorous, and entertaining—and they provide the perfect opportunity to tease and torment the jittery pair. Themes are based on the couple's mutual interests and pastimes, talents and skills, personality traits, or occupations.

Trends
- His 'n' Hers wedding showers usually take place at locations that reflect the couple's interests: golf courses, bowling alleys, art galleries, shopping malls, sports events, or even places of employment.

Tips
- Consult the couple's friends or family members if you have any doubts about the appropriateness of your theme. It would be quite disappointing if any of your plans insulted or embarrassed the couple.
- Plan a potluck event. Coordinate a menu of the couple's favorite foods and beverages; then present the couple with all the recipes bound into a booklet.
- Collect bits of advice from all the guests. Write the advice on index cards, and present them in a decorative box to the couple. If you do this before the party, the couple can read the advice out loud as a party activity.

Twists
Consider the following themes for a couple's wedding shower:
- Wedding Ceremony: A hilarious shower theme in which guests dress to represent members of a wedding party and act out all phases of a wedding day, exaggerating and embellishing each phase to put a real fright into the couple of honor. The "ceremony" could include the exchange of irreverent vows, and everybody could listen to and/or sing such songs as "Stand By Your Man," "The Impossible Dream," and "What Kind of Fool Am I?" This zany fun is a must video opportunity!
- White Elephant: Also an incredibly funny theme in which guests bring the most gosh-awful items, wrapped as serious gifts, and seriously present them to the couple. After the laughter dies down, the couple receives the real gifts.
- Party: Guests bring a variety of party supplies to stock an Instant Party Kit for the happy couple to use when they want to celebrate at the mere drop of a party hat. This theme is ideal for couples known as the "hosts with the most," as well as for a pair of party-giving novices.

 For other themes appropriate for your occasion, see the theme grid on page 188.

BACHELOR/
BACHELORETTE PARTIES

A bachelor/bachelorette party can be fun, funny, rowdy, and even risqué, yet planned with a degree of dignity. Since the party takes place just a few days before the wedding, it is advisable to avoid activities that will harm the health or reputation of the intended, if you get my drift!

Trends
- A prenuptial celebration for a bride or groom can vary greatly, from a sophisticated cigar-and-whiskey dinner (an event that has recently become more than acceptable for women) to a beer-and-burger bash at the local pub. Limousine club tours, strippers or strip joints, poker games, and all-night gab fests are all accepted components of a stag/stagette party. The personality of the bachelor/bachelorette pretty much determines the plan.
- Guys and gals can both enjoy a favorite activity, such as bowling, skating, golf, or tennis, followed by cocktails, food, and humorous bachelor/bachelorette roasting, dishing of advice, and story telling about the guest(s) of honor.

Tips
- Roast and toast the bachelor/bachelorette in a traditional banquet setting, dais and all. Show embarrassing photos, videos, or movies, accompanied by appropriate commentary. Videotape the entire event, and use it as blackmail, or give it as a wedding gift—to the mate.
- Find out whether the bachelor/bachelorette likes to gamble. If yes, organize a trip to a casino, or have a casino-theme party at your own home. A gambling theme is particularly fitting, since the guest of honor will be taking a very big gamble in a few days. Give the winnings, if any, to the guest of honor.

Twists
For Him:
- Plan a Tool Time stag party, honoring the nation's number-one goof-off husband and work-bench wonder, Tim Allen. Guests in plaid shirts or work clothes watch rerun videos, play cards, drink a few beers (getting "hammered" is optional), and give the guest of honor a few sage words of advice on marriage—over the back fence, of course.

For Her:
- Use a fortune-telling theme for the party, complete with a card, tea leaf, handwriting, or palm reader. Blend the mystical with food and beverages, add a touch of gossip and giggling, and total success is predicted.
- Throw a Pampering Party. While sharing wedding horror stories, well-wishes, and a bottle or two of champagne, the guests give each other manicures, pedicures, and facials. Hire a professional masseuse to give the bride-to-be a luxurious massage.

For other themes appropriate for your occasion, see the theme grid on page 188.

WEDDING RECEPTION

Theme parties often replace traditional wedding reception banquets. Blending the traditions of a wedding ceremony with the trends of a unique reception can be a challenge, but the result will please the members of the wedding party and the guests as well.

Trends
- Wedding reception themes are usually based upon the following: travel destinations, occupations, special interests and hobbies, talents, ethnic backgrounds, couple's first meeting, or anything that is of great significance to the bride and groom. You may want to incorporate a theme, even if it is a whimsical one, into a semiformal gathering. And themes of any kind are extremely effective when planned for a casual gathering.

Tips
- Decide upon a theme, and follow it for the food, room decor, activities, favors, music, and entertainment, if possible. The more details you design into your plan, the easier for the guests to get right into the swing of things.
- Prepare a special dining/activity area for small children, if needed. Decorate the area with balloons, streamers, and colorful tableware. Plan special party favors and activities for the youngsters. You may want to hire a teenage child or sibling of an invited guest to oversee the younger children. This extra expense may easily be covered by serving the children a kids' meal of hot dogs or hamburgers instead of a more expensive entrée, which they probably wouldn't eat anyway.
- On the RSVP card, include a question about the age of child(ren) attending, so you can prepare for the above suggestion. (See Party Tips, #5, for more advice on kids at weddings.)

Twists
- Decorate the enclosure reception cards according to the theme. For example: a tiny silk flower to indicate a tropical luau, a tiny flag to denote an ethnic celebration, a sticker or drawing of a 45 record to herald a fifties fling.
- Continue the party theme for take-home favors. For example: a Hawaiian ti plant (a tropical, green shrub) wrapped in cellophane and trimmed with a sea shell for a luau; a small bottle of Italian spices tied with red, white, and green ribbons for an Italian celebration; a novelty Coca Cola refrigerator magnet attached to a Coke can holding a small bunch of flowers for a fifties party.

For other themes appropriate for your occasion, see the theme grid on page 188.

GIFT OPENING

This event, held late in the morning after the wedding, has become more popular in recent years—since it provides an opportunity to not only open gifts, but to rehash and reminisce about the previous day's events. In addition, this event also provides a special time for out-of-town guests to gather for their last farewells.

Trends
- This event is very casual and laid-back, usually held before noon, with folks coming and going at their own convenience.
- It is the ideal time for the bride and groom to make a special presentation of gifts or speeches of gratitude to their parents, to people who have helped immensely in the wedding, and to people who invested time and money (for travel and hotel) to attend the wedding.

Tips
- Save expensive paper and ribbons to reuse in the future.
- Serve a buffet of leftovers from the wedding, along with a Continental breakfast or brunch fare.
- Videotape the event, especially the gift opening, with critiques and compliments from all the guests. You will enjoy the fun and frolic for years to come.
- Watch some of the video taken at the wedding and reception. Send selected video clips to VIPs unable to attend the wedding.
- Keep careful track of who gave what, for the thank-you notes.

Twists
- Send thank-you notes in envelopes made from the wrapping paper of the people's gifts.
- Keep all the wedding greeting cards you receive. A year later, turn those greeting cards into postcards, and mail them back to the sender, with the message, "We're thinking of you as we recall the joy of our wedding day. Thank you again for making it so special!" (See Party How-To's, #17.)
- Take instant photos of the couple with gifts received from absent guests. Send photos along with thank-you notes and, if possible, party favors.

FIRST ANNIVERSARY

Making it through the first year of marriage, with all of its tests and adjustments, is a perfect reason to celebrate. Besides, the top layer of wedding cake that is still in the freezer must be eaten. Couples tend to see this event as private, but they will usually be complimented if you expand the party to include a few friends and family members.

Trends
- A special brunch, dinner, or evening of dessert and coffee is dedicated to celebrate the milestone. This event may be planned at the host's home, at a favorite restaurant, or at any place that has special meaning to the couple.
- The official gift for the first anniversary is paper.

Tips
- Use the actual invitation, program, party favors, and decorations used on the wedding day, or duplicate them for the party. (See Party Tips, #1.)
- Place White Elephant gifts (see Couple's Wedding Shower, the Twists section, page 16) around the room for party decor. White Elephant gifts are those that people usually hide in the deepest, darkest corner of the closet, and bring out only when the giver of the gift visits.
- Suggest that guests wear the outfits they wore to the wedding.
- Create such meaningful party favors as a wedding photo of the guest(s) with the happy couple. Improvise if such a photo does not exist (cutting and pasting may be necessary).

Twists
- Show the wedding video. Arrange theater-style seating, and serve popcorn and cold drinks. Instead of having guests bring gifts, set up a concession booth of candy and ice cream (sold at slightly boosted prices); then give the cash to the anniversary couple, to use for a romantic dinner for two. Money qualifies as an official gift for the first anniversary: paper.
- Create a quiz made up of questions about the wedding day, including names of guests, menu items, activities, and interesting events. Have the anniversary couple write their answers separately; then read the answers aloud for a bunch of laughs.
- Play The Newlywed Game to test the memories, intuition, and communication skills of all couples at the party.

TENTH ANNIVERSARY

A couple that celebrates ten years of marriage, and perhaps children, is usually more than ready to get away for a weekend (or more) of romantic "relationship rejuvenation." Friends and family can put their heads together and plan an anniversary party with a "send-off to the weekend" theme.

Trends
- This party is not unlike the couple's wedding shower, with its theme of romance and humor. The purpose, along with celebrating, is to pump a shot of excitement and recollection of "how-it-was-then" into the relationship. Music, dress, and decor can reflect the fashions popular ten years ago.
- The official gifts for the tenth anniversary are tin and aluminum.

Tips
- Give gag gifts. The degree to which the gifts are romantic or risqué should be left to the discretion of the gift-giver. This party is definitely for adults.
- Have the anniversary couple take a zany written quiz about their married life; then read both sets of answers aloud for comparison.
- Play a few raucous rounds of The Newlywed Game to put all the couples on the spot and to provide a lively and spirited activity.

Twists
- Tell the guests to wear nighties, robes, or pj's befitting a honeymoon night.
- Have the guests wear bridesmaids' dresses and groomsmen's tuxedos (no rule as to gender choice) from the era of the anniversary couple's wedding.
- Conduct a wedding ceremony with hilarious, custom-written, updated vows.
- Give the anniversary couple a humorous hint of what they might expect on their romantic getaway: Serve a romantic meal with champagne on an elegant tray, with fresh flowers for the bride and groom, and create a romantic atmosphere of candlelight and soft music. After a short time of quiet uninterrupted conversation, loudly bring them back to reality with kids' noises (if applicable), ringing telephones, and pet ruckus. Simultaneously, snatch away their deluxe tray and replace it with a TV dinner—in other words, create a slice of real life. Add a six-pack of beer to that TV dinner, and you've got a mighty appropriate gift for the tin and aluminum anniversary.
- Glue or solder a shiny dime to a shiny safety pin, and present each guest with their own "dime and pin" as a perfect tenth anniversary favor.

For other themes appropriate for your occasion, see the theme grid on page 188.

TWENTY-FIFTH ANNIVERSARY

Silver, both the color and the metal, is the theme, which provides wonderful opportunities for beautiful party decor. At this celebration, the couple's friends, family, and memories are the most cherished treasures. A party that takes all three into consideration will be a major, sterling-silver hit.

Trends
- Most couples celebrating twenty-five years of marriage will likely have children and grandchildren to include in the festivities, so family-oriented parties are popular.
- In some social circles, adults-only dinner parties are also quite popular. Usually, these circles have a traditional way in which to celebrate this milestone.

Tips
- Use the anniversary couple's shared interests or pastimes, ethnic backgrounds, or interesting personal facts to establish a party theme.
- Recreate the wedding day—this theme works well for family and adults-only celebrations. At a family gathering, have the children also come dressed as members of the wedding party. Even the family pet can don a bow tie or a fancy hair bow.
- Use the destination or mode of travel planned by the couple for a special anniversary trip as an excellent theme for the party.
- Pool resources to buy one special gift for the anniversary couple. A silver tray upon which the names of all guests have been engraved makes a nice gift. Or give a silver vase filled with a huge silk-flower bouquet created by combining individual blossoms brought by each guest or couple.
- Play a wedding trivia game: Divide the guests into teams, and give each team a quiz sheet and a pen. Have the teams complete the quiz quickly and correctly. Once everybody is finished, read the answers aloud. Be prepared for enthusiastic competitiveness.

Twists
- Plan a wedding-ceremony-reenactment party, with formal invitations, floral decorations, and balloons. Announce arriving guests; set up an altar/archway for photo opportunities; serve a reception menu on decorated tables; follow through with traditional wedding-dance antics; and give the guests a festive farewell by attaching tin cans and old shoes to their automobile back bumpers.
- Present the anniversary couple with $25 gift certificates (the guests' combined budget will determine the number of certificates) to a favorite restaurant, or twenty-five passes to various activities, such as movies or video rentals.
- Hand out theme-appropriate party favors, such as small, silver photo frames or silver-dollar small magnets.

For other themes appropriate for your occasion, see the theme grid on page 188.

FIFTIETH ANNIVERSARY

Regardless of whether you choose gold medals, gold doubloons, or Golden Arches to be the party motif, a fiftieth anniversary party must include grand touches of 24-karat gold. Enhance all aspects of the celebration by adding the Midas touch.

Trends
- Whether planning a gala dinner party or an afternoon open house planned around the anniversary couple's interests, hobbies, talents, skills, ethnic backgrounds, or personalities—the event is generously dusted with gold, humor, and sentiment.

Tips
- Provide all guests with a sheet of blank music paper. Have each guest write a message, poem, or special tribute to the anniversary couple, or tell them to attach a significant photo to the sheet. Then ask everybody to head the sheet with a song title that reminds them of the couple. Place all sheets into a master book (covered in gold fabric) for an incredibly meaningful gift.
- Create a videotaped record of the party, including special messages to the anniversary couple from all the guests.

Twists
See the following popular fiftieth-anniversary themes:
- Golden Garden Gala: Guests acknowledge the couple's love for each other and for gardening and flowers by planning the invitations, decor, favors, and food to reflect the garden theme. Each guest brings one silk flower that becomes part of a lavish bouquet presented to the couple in a lovely, crystal, gold-trimmed vase.
- Big-Band Bash: Music- and dance-lovers pay tribute to the music and dances that were popular fifty years ago—at the time of the couple's wedding. Costumes, music, entertainment, decor, and food all match the theme.
- Trip Down Memory Lane: Couples who have lived in the same town for many years celebrate their anniversary by taking a "moving-through-time" bus tour of significant places. A bit of refreshment and/or entertainment is offered at each stop—perhaps even a surprise guest or two.
- Let's Say It Again: The couple renews their wedding vows in a real or simulated ceremony, as applicable. Guests receive formal invitations and may dress as part of the wedding party. The wedding reception is designed to repeat the reception of fifty years ago, including traditional toasts, cake cutting, garter and bouquet throwing.

For other themes appropriate for your occasion, see the theme grid on page 188.

BABY SHOWER

Showering the mom-to-be with sweet little gifts or practical big gifts for the new baby is a wonderful tradition. Themes, decor, food, and entertainment are usually light and bright. However, these days hostesses are getting highly creative and elaborate with their plans.

Trends

- In the past one might have said, "I have to go to a baby shower," but these days, the phrase has become, "I get to go to a baby shower." The creativity and enthusiasm of the hostess(es), combined with the great variety of readily available party supplies, are the reasons for the changing attitudes.
- Baby showers can be held morning, noon, or night; indoors or outdoors; in a private home, at work, at a public place, or on the move. They can involve the mom-to-be in the planning, or be planned as a surprise, to add a little extra excitement. (See Resources, #41, 58, for more ideas.)

Tips

- Encourage the guest of honor to register at a big discount store, especially a chain store. This will widen the selection of gifts, enable guests from out-of-state to easily choose presents, and allow the shoppers to benefit from reduced prices.
- Consider having guests bring "like-new" baby items, as well as new ones. This is an excellent way to recycle and reuse treasured garments and toys. (You may want to check with the guest of honor about this.)
- Make sure that all the guests RSVP. You may want to follow the example of one hostess who ensured 100 percent response to her invitation. She left off the date of the party—by accident.

Twists

See the following popular themes for baby showers:

- Garage Sale (for the bargain-hunter mom-to-be): Guests buy gifts at thrift or consignment stores or at garage sales—the gifts must be new or like new. Tell the guests to wrap the gifts, but to leave on the low price tag. The guest of honor will be thrilled to see the prices and to know that because of them she got three times the volume of gifts. Invitations, decor, and refreshments should reflect this "recycling" theme.
- A variation on the Garage Sale theme: Everybody goes garage sale shopping, and the guest of honor is given an unlimited shopping budget. After shopping, everybody returns to the host's house for lunch and inspection of the great haul.
- Gift Certificate: Guests give certificates for pampering services to the guest of honor—to be fulfilled by the guest or a professional.
- Smart Baby: Guests give educational toys and parenting or children's books and videos to the mom-to-be.

For other themes appropriate for your occasion, see the theme grid on page 188.

COUPLE'S BABY SHOWER

Celebrating the upcoming birth of a child, especially a first child, has traditionally been a "women's" thing, but the current trend is to include the expectant father and other male guests in the festivities. These coed showers have become very popular; often they are full-blown parties set to innovative themes.

Trends

- Coed baby showers are usually planned around a theme related to the occupations, interests, talents, or lifestyle of the pregnant couple.
- Roasts and spoofs, with gag gifts as well as practical items, are ideal for couple's baby showers.
- Coed showers now take place in venues of shared interest to the couple. Examples: golf course, bowling alley, art gallery, shopping mall, baseball field, or place of employment, if possible.

Tips

- Consider a potluck-style event. If guests share the food expenses, you will have extra funds for a more-elaborate party.
- Be prepared with loaded cameras—regular, instant, and video. The photographic documentation of the goings-on at these exuberant and laugh-filled occasions are priceless. (See Resources, #58, for game ideas.)
- Tape guests' advice on parenting.
- Videotape guest interviews and wishes to the new baby. Ask questions about Mom and Dad and the funny things they have been doing in preparation for the baby's arrival.

Twists

See the following popular themes for couple's baby showers:

- Time Capsule: Guests bring gifts that document the day and/or year: newspapers, video clips of the TV news, best-selling books, popular musical recordings, and so on. Pack the items and a videotaped interview of all guests into a canister, to be preserved and enjoyed by the happy family. In addition to the capsule gifts, the guests should pool their money to buy one serious gift.
- Here's to the Future (a hot, coed baby shower theme): Guests choose gifts that are state-of-the-art, modernistic, or space age—any computer or high-tech gadgets fit into these categories. This theme is especially successful for computer/Internet/Web enthusiasts. The food, decor, activities, and party favors should all follow the *Year 2000, Star Trek*, or Space Exploration themes.

For other themes appropriate for your occasion, see the theme grid on page 188.

HIGH-SCHOOL GRADUATION

These days, getting through twelve grades can be a challenge for young people. So, by showing a graduate our appreciation and admiration, we encourage him or her to continue the bright path of education. There's no better way to say "'Atta Way!" than with a TGIG (Thank God I Graduated) bash.

Trends
- A graduation party is most often an open house or a full-fledged party set to a theme of the graduate's interests or talents—sports, music, science, art, drama, or today's big one—electronics and computers. Any of these will provide a good basis for an appealing party theme for guests of all ages.

Tips
- Think about any dream or goal the graduate may have. Perhaps the graduate dreams of traveling. Use the dream or goal to create a wonderful, personal party theme.
- Consider the ages and interests of your guests. For example, if the party is for "kids" only, one activity theme, such as bowling, skating, swimming, or volleyball, will be popular. However, if both adults and younger children will attend, a casual, outdoor get-together with a variety of activities, such as competitions and games, will occupy and entertain all guests.

Twists
See the following popular themes for graduation parties:
- Comedy: All the guests wear fake arrows through their heads and horn-rimmed glasses with mustaches and funny noses. Go all out with dribble glasses, Whoopee Cushions, and so on.
- Pizza, Pasta, and Pictionary: Guests pile their choice of toppings onto a pizza crust, totally pig out on pizza and pasta, and then play Pictionary.
- Treasure or Scavenger Hunt. (See Party Tactics, page 160.)
- Karaoke/Star Search. (See page 92.)
- Circus, Circus. (See page 86.) This party will appease all those graduates who are thinking of running away to a life under the Big Top.

For other themes appropriate for your occasion, see the theme grid on page 188.

COLLEGE GRADUATION

Hip, hip, hooray! A great accomplishment calls for a great celebration. Celebrate with a gathering of family, friends, and classmates. Whether the graduate is now a B.A., M.S., Ph.D., M.D., Esq., or D.D.S., it's time to P.A.R.T.Y!

Trends
- The occupation that the graduate will follow is always an ideal theme for the party. Design everything from the invitation to the thank-you note accordingly.
- In addition to the standard friends-and-family open-house celebration, the party may also be a large theme gala, a classmates-only picnic outing, or an intimate formal family dinner at a fancy restaurant. In other words, anything goes.

Tips
- Know the difference between a graduation announcement and an invitation. If you want someone to attend the ceremony or celebration, you must invite them with a short note or card inserted into the announcement.
- Never use form-letter thank-you notes for graduation gifts or acknowledgments. Always write a personal note.
- Give special instructions for drinking policy. Most of the guest-of-honor's classmates will be of age, but take precautions for underage guests. The host is fully responsible for any accident that involves a driver to whom the host has given alcoholic beverages.

Twists
- Throw a "Soon-to-Be-a-Lawyer" party for a law-school-bound graduate. Write invitations on legal pad sheets or design them to look and read as a subpoena; use scales of justice and gavels as part of the decor; play a name-tag mixer game of legalese trivia (see Party Tips, #7); and dress the bartender as a judge and stand him or her behind a bar designed as a judicial bench.
- Keep in mind that not all graduates choose a profession or continue on to graduate school immediately upon graduation. The following two party themes are generic enough for any graduation party:
  —Hats Off to [graduate] (in keeping with the tradition of throwing the graduation cap in the air): On the invitations, draw a square graduation cap that is floating in the air, and suggest that each guest wear a hat that best depicts their personality. During the party, create instant hilarity by having guests swap hats each time a bell rings. Use hats in the party decor and as food containers. Present minihats on key chains as take-home favors.
  —Job Hunting: Design a postcard invitation using a fake employment agency logo, and instruct the guests to search the Help Wanted column in the local newspaper for a voice-mail number. Record an RSVP message with pertinent party information, using the sixties hit "Get a Job" as background music. Ask the guests to come dressed for their dream job. Decorate with employment-related posters, career advertisements, job applications, enlarged want ads, and tools of various trades.

For other themes appropriate for your occasion, see the theme grid on page 188.

GOING AWAY/MOVING

Going-away celebrations are really Bad News/Good News parties. While it is always sad to have someone leave us, in most cases the guest of honor is moving to bigger and better things. These parties should be meaningful and sentimental, but still upbeat and cheerful.

Trends
- All party details, such as decorations, food, dress, entertainment, prizes, and favors, are most often planned around the guest-of-honor's destination or around a general traveling theme.
- Potluck parties let guests share the expense of the refreshments. You can apply the potluck strategy to food, beverages, decorations, music, and so on.
- Going-away parties are frequently planned as surprise parties.

Tips
- Send the invitations in small boxes with excelsior packing. (See Party Tips, #2.)
- Instruct guests to come dressed ready to move or travel, or in costume appropriate to the guest-of-honor's destination.
- Provide all guests with envelopes, stamps, and pens, and have each guest self-address and stamp envelopes. Present these envelopes to the guest of honor as a reminder to keep in touch.
- Consider the following gift ideas:
  —A beautifully drawn map of the "home" city. Use shiny stars to mark the location of each guest's home. Frame the finished product and present it to the guest of honor in a packing box.
  —A videotape of farewell speeches. For an extra-special memento, add video-taped memories from past activities—you may need special equipment for this.
  —An album filled with memory pages, one designed by each guest, that include written messages, drawings, photos, and decorative touches.
  —A globe on which the destination and departure sites are marked with decorative push pins. Link the push pins together with a gold cord or chain.

Twists
- Plan a couple's going-away party to pay tribute to Bonnie and Clyde—a two-some famous for quick getaways. Create a Wanted poster invitation that reads "They're stealing our hearts."
- Play a name-tag game in which guests match song, book, or movie titles that have a travel theme (songs such as "On the Road Again" and "Leaving on a Jet Plane," movies such as *Airplane* or *Orient Express*, and so on) to the recording artist, author, or lead actors. (See Party Tips, #4, 7.)
- Conduct a sing-along of farewell songs. Hand out song sheets to which you have stapled tissues.

NEW HOME/ HOUSE WARMING

In this party, the proud new home owners throw open their doors and roll out the red carpet to introduce friends and family to their new digs. For the most part, this is an informal gathering, although you can use a theme to plan this party, if you like.

Trends
- Innovative hosts may use the neighborhood, the name of the street, or the style in which the home is decorated as a theme for the party.

Tips
- Remember that the host must never ask for gifts! One hostess brazenly told her guests where she was registered! WRONG! Then again, telling the guests, "No gifts, please" is actually inhospitable, because guests will want to bring a small token of good luck. Don't mention gifts at all, and just let things happen.
- Consider the following gift ideas: address labels, door knocker, nameplate, wine, imprinted napkins, gift certificates to neighborhood merchants, framed or preserved invitation, plants, a subscription to a home decorating magazine.

Twists
- Design the party around a Dedication Ceremony theme: Send a formal invitation that says, "Join us for the dedication ceremony of _____." Serve cocktails and appetizers on the front lawn. Conduct a formal ceremony including a ribbon cutting, a proclamation of good luck, and a presentation of a huge key to the new home. Enlist the talents of a high-school brass section for tribute music. Print a small brochure introducing features of the new home, and schedule mock tours every hour.
- Consider a Treasure Hunt theme: Write the party information on a treasure map, with instructions for guests to make a few stops to find small gifts and/or refreshments along the way. As the guests arrive at your home, give them gold-medal name tags for completing the hunt. Continue the treasure theme with such party details as small wooden chests filled with snacks, gold and silver lamé table covers, jeweled napkin rings, bowls filled with faux jewelry, and bags of chocolate gold coins as party favors.
- Be bold and daring. Of course, hosts want their new home to look picture perfect for the party, but wouldn't it be a kick to leave the rooms filled with packing boxes and furniture stacked in the middle? As a party activity, have the guests unpack boxes and arrange furniture, as assigned. The reward for completing this task is a party.

For other themes appropriate for your occasion, see the theme grid on page 188.

BON VOYAGE/ VACATION

Party guests at a festive Bon Voyage send-off can share the anticipation and excitement of an upcoming trip, without sharing the expense, time investment, or in the case of a cruise, sea sickness that may accompany the actual trip. Since one rarely gets the chance to take a cruise or an international trip, one mustn't pass up the chance to "voyage vicariously" with the help of a bon voyage party.

Trends
- Bon voyage/vacation parties have a built-in theme—the trip itself, such as a cruise, or the final destination. All party details should follow the chosen theme: the decor, food, music, and entertainment.

Tips
- Send invitations in passport-style mailers, airline folders, or travel brochures.
- Use props to create settings typical of the mode of travel. For example, cruise ship decor must include deck chairs, life preservers, and nautical equipment.
- Use cardboard to build a 4-by-6-foot stateroom, without a porthole—as an example of a "luxurious" stateroom the traveler may encounter.
- Decorate the party site with travel posters and giant postcards. (See Party How-To's, #7.)
- Create small vacation sets/scenes, such as sidewalk cafés, art galleries, quaint shops, and shady, palm-covered seating areas.
- Ask guests to dress in cruise wear, as crew members, or as natives of the destination.
- Greet guests with the *Love Boat* theme or other music typical of the destination.
- Serve foods representing ship, train, or airplane menus, or destination favorites.
- Give silly or practical gifts for the guest(s) of honor to take on the trip.

Twists
- Set up a cruise ship backdrop for souvenir photos, including a sign that says "SS (guest-of-honor's name)." Create backdrops or prop settings for other vacation plans, such as a plane, train, or even automobile.
- Have guests fill out generic picture postcards addressed to their friends and families. Give these cards to the guest of honor, who will then mail them from various ports or from the final destination. The recipients of these cards will be very puzzled by the sender's ability to slip away on a trip without missing a day of work. This party activity will extend the enjoyment of the party for the guests.

For other themes appropriate for your occasion, see the theme grid on page 188.

RETIREMENT

For some people, retirement is not a joyful concept—they would rather keep working at something they love. Then again, others can't wait to punch a time card for the last time. Knowing and respecting your retiree's true feelings is essential when planning a personal and meaningful party.

Trends
- A party that uses loafing, lolling, twiddling thumbs, and napping all day as its themes isn't as appropriate as it once was. Retirees have plans! Plans for activities and adventures that may involve more exertion than the job they are leaving.
- Usually, coworkers are the ones who honor the business accomplishments of a retiree at a farewell banquet or dinner. Family members, however, have the pleasure of planning a festive gathering to launch the retiree into a brand new life of doing whatever he or she darn well pleases.
- Party plans range from very simple to moderately elaborate to a "thememania" extravaganza. Whatever the scope, go for it.

Tips
- Have guests bring gifts (real or gag) that will fill the retiree's spare time: books, tapes, hobby supplies, tools, games, or pillows.
- Choose a party theme that focuses away from work and onto retiree's hobbies, interests, goals, or aspirations: traveling, gardening, doing home improvements, fishing, writing, reading, or cooking.
- Consider the following list of favors and prizes: faux gold watches, retiree's old business cards with printed instructions on ways to use them (toothpicks, table-leg de-wobblers, bookmarks, fingernail cleaners, and so on), job-site souvenirs, job-related garments or uniforms, or office supplies wrapped as prizes.

Twists
- Plan the party around the Leisure Time theme:
  —For the invitations, send "Do Not Disturb" signs with party details printed on the back, faux paychecks "To bearer...for being a great guest," or time cards that say "Punching out for good."
  —Request that guests dress in their lazying-around clothes and carry any matching gear or equipment (fishing rod, garden tools, and so on).
  —Arrange lounge chairs, hammocks, chaise lounges, pillows, footstools, and rocking chairs for guest seating.
  —Park an RV in your driveway, if possible; and decorate the site with retirement posters, travel ads, and relaxation equipment (scuba gear, skis).
  —Create a "typical retirement day" calendar, noting such important activities as bingo, horseshoes, napping, looking at one's own navel, and asking, "When are we going to eat again?" Blow it up to poster-size for all to enjoy.
  —Choose your own menu, or serve typical cafeteria food on trays. Serve snacks out of lunch pails or brown bags.

For other themes appropriate for your occasion, see the theme grid on page 188.

MEMORIAL SERVICE

Speaking from my own experience, commemorating the life of a dearly departed with a festive memorial service can be a meaningful and healing process. Your family will know the right thing to do, and whether the event is a wake, a jazz wake, a Shiva, or a memorial service, it will be a fabulous, fond-farewell celebration.

Trends
- Guests gather to pay tribute to and celebrate the life of a loved one with speeches, songs, poems, photos, and memorabilia.
- The plans for a memorial celebration are extremely personal and individual. For the planners, anything that seems appropriate, goes.
- The celebration can take place in a hall, auditorium, private dining room, party room, private home, or at a site as unconventional as a baseball field.

Tips
- Send an invitation just as you would for any other celebration.
- Allow anyone to attend, with no restriction or limitations. Guests are not only there for themselves, but also for the survivors.
- Make sure that all family members agree on such details as program, music, decor, and refreshments.

Twists
- Decide on an appropriate day for this event: you can schedule it shortly after the death, or postpone it until a special date, such as a birthday or anniversary.

Note: The following is how my family celebrated the memorial service for my father: We selected a site that had a lot of personal meaning to my whole family. The hall was decorated with balloons, streamers, flowers, and plants. One friend played a guitar, another friend read aloud special messages written by the adult children, and grown grandchildren sang special solos. A favorite clergyman presented a short memorial. We had a slide show of a lifetime of photos, shown along with background music of Kenny Rogers' song "Through the Years." All guests joined in on a sing-along of Mom and Dad's favorite song ("Sentimental Journey"), the words to which were printed on the program. Food and drink, more music, and socializing completed a memorial celebration that my dear father would have loved. In fact, I am sure, did love.

 For other themes appropriate for your occasion, see the theme grid on page 188.

FAMILY REUNIONS

A family reunion of any size should be designed to encourage sharing of stories, getting acquainted with new members, updating address books and genealogical records, and, all through the reunion, reminiscing.

Trends

- A huge family reunion is planned two to three years in advance, in order to locate and notify everyone. Organizations are available that will plan your whole reunion for you, or simply help you find family members. (See Resources, # 59.)
- Local family reunions require less lead time, and will most likely be small enough to take place in a backyard.
- A reunion weekend's schedule should allow ample time for visiting and reminiscing. Ideally, it would include the following elements:
    —Welcoming/registration area for Friday afternoon and evening arrivals;
    —"Open almost all hours" hospitality area where guests can gather for impromptu reuniting and meetings;
    —Saturday morning Continental breakfast;
    —Block of open time Saturday afternoon for sightseeing and/or visiting local friends;
    —Picnic or party on Saturday evening (some diehards will continue the party after-hours in the hospitality area);
    —Sunday morning church services (when applicable);
    —Farewell brunch.

Tips

- Send an initial mailing to survey preferences for dates/locations/types of events, to give the guests an opportunity to voice any special requests, and to obtain updates on personal information and missing addresses. Then use this information as a planning guide.
- Send a printed summary of family news to all who make reservations. Before guests arrive at the event, they can familiarize themselves with names, mates, marriages, divorces, births, and deaths. In addition, you may want to provide data on employment, occupations, hobbies, and other tidbits of personal information. This minibriefing removes initial awkwardness and makes the actual time of reuniting more comfortable.
- Hire a professional, I repeat, *professional* videographer to tape interviews of attendees, especially of the elderly guests, at the Saturday afternoon event. The showing of this tape on Saturday evening will be the highlight of your weekend. Profits from selling copies to family members will usually pay for the video's production.
- Choose a gathering place that corresponds to the size of your group. While smaller groups may be perfectly comfortable at your home, you may want to hold larger group gatherings at a park, a farmyard, or even a resort.

For other themes appropriate for your occasion, see the theme grid on page 188.   **33**

- Take the time to research overnight accommodations for out-of-town guests. Rooms rented at private homes or in college dormitories may be less expensive than standard hotel accommodations.
- Keep expenses down for out-of-town guests (who already have travel and lodging expenses). Most of the events should be inexpensive, potluck, or hosted by local family members.
- Pay extra attention to plans for children. Entertain and occupy youngsters with simple and inexpensive activities, games, contests, and prizes. If the budget allows, give each child a visor or hat on which you have written the child's name and reason for award (for example: First prize in the jumping jack contest). (See Resources, #20.)

Twists

- Arrange for part or all of the event to take place at a site that has historical meaning to the family.
- Feature "family" dishes in all event menus. Then print copies of all recipes and give to each family member as a memento.
- Give each guest a few envelopes addressed to the reunion organizer, and tell them to use the envelopes to report any interesting news or changes in their family. Use this information, along with photos of the event, to publish a family reunion-update newsletter.

 For other themes appropriate for your occasion, see the theme grid on page 188.

CLASS REUNIONS

Having attended and planned too many reunions to mention, I can tell you that the committees have more fun before the actual reunion than all of the attendees at the reunion put together. So join the planning committee, and you'll have a ball helping to plan your high-school or college reunion.

Trends

- Reunions tend to be a whole-weekend event, which includes the following elements: an optional get-together at a nostalgic spot on Friday evening, a pre-reunion gathering at or near the event site on Saturday, and a closing brunch and/or picnic on Sunday. This plan gives attendees several chances to socialize with their classmates. A typical four-hour dinner party is just not enough.
- Reunions are being planned with such themes as The Forties, The Fifties, The Sixties, and The Seventies—usually, the decade of the graduation. Costumes, music, decor, and activities follow the theme to really take the guests back in time.
- The school's motto or theme is, of course, also a common party theme. For instance, our class was the Cowboys, so our reunion party was a good-old-fashioned hoedown.

Tips

- Keep three factors in mind: 1) The reunion planners' goal is to get the best turnout possible. 2) The reason people go to a reunion is to spend time with classmates, not to eat an expensive meal. 3) For many classmates, cost is a deciding factor. If you can charge half as much money by serving a hearty sandwich buffet rather than a sit-down dinner, you will greatly increase your turnout.
- Send an early postcard questionnaire to update the mailing list, get commitments for help, and get classmates' feedback on dates for the event, type of event, and attendance plans.
- Use the postcard response to help you decide upon the type of event and location, to estimate the turnout, to plan the budget, and to set the cost per person.
- Keep careful track of returned postcards, and set up a resourceful and persistent "bloodhound" committee to search for missing persons.
- Decide whether the event will take place at a hotel. If yes, negotiate for a special rate on the event room. Also try to negotiate room rates for out-of-town guests.
- Send out invitations. To get an enthusiastic response, your invitation must be attractive (preferably professionally designed), free of typos, neatly addressed, and include all vital information. If possible, include an SASE to ensure that all reservations reach you.
- Enclose a form with the invitations to collect data for your reunion directory. Make sure to provide ample space for the answers. (The last form of this kind I saw asked for "interesting comments," but only provided two two-inch lines. Not nearly enough for all my interesting news!) If you like, invite classmates to promote their businesses in the reunion directory.

For other themes appropriate for your occasion, see the theme grid on page 188.   **35**

- Wait a few weeks, then follow up the invitations with postcards to those who have not responded. Or put the phone committee to work calling for responses. An enthusiastic caller can actually sell people on attending.
- Once all reservations and information sheets are in, your committee can create those laugh-getting name tags that feature yearbook photos.
- Hire a desktop publisher (or find someone on the committee who is handy with a basic desktop publishing program) and prepare the data for your directory. The directory doesn't have to be expensive or fancy, just neat and easy to read.
- Hire a professional videographer to tape mini-interviews with classmates. Save the tape to show at the next reunion, and offer to sell copies to anyone who is interested. Keep in mind that although you may have a classmate volunteer to do the taping, a guaranteed-quality product requires a professional.
- Review all aspects of the party planning approximately two weeks before the event: Double-check caterer and party-room guarantees, check on the progress of the decoration and/or entertainment committee(s), and confirm any other services, such as photographer or videographer.

Twists

- Solicit donations of products and services from your classmates and use them to barter on needed items, such as music, decorations, printing, mailing, prizes, photographer, and videographer.
- Print an inexpensive "cheat sheet" of classmates' personal data, and send it to all those who will attend. This information will give classmates a sneak peek at the classmates they will encounter at the reunion.
- Consider planning a minireunion. In an off-year (our twenty-seventh) we reserved the banquet room of a popular night club that included a deejay, an appetizer buffet, and an open bar for one hour. We sent a simple postcard invitation three weeks prior to the event. Even though the party was given on short notice, we had a great response. Attendees' feedback indicated that the party was easy to attend, and that the total cost of $18 per person was pleasantly inexpensive. Many still say that, although brief, it was the best reunion ever. It was definitely the best attended. Consider gathering your classmates more frequently, at a lower cost. These minievents will keep your class closer, especially after the twenty-fifth.

NEIGHBORHOOD BLOCK PARTY

Every summer, thousands of neighbors block off their streets and kick up their heels at rollicking block parties planned for past, present, and future residents. Adults, kids, and pets show up to eat, drink, play, and catch up on the latest news and gossip.

Trends
- More often than not, the block party is planned with one of the following themes: Luau, Sportathon, Circus, Western, State Fair, or Tacky/Tasteless.
- The planning committee meets months ahead to do some initial research among the guests, to design the plan, and then to set it in motion.
- Many groups add an altruistic element by using the party to raise money or collect goods for charity.
- If weather plays a trick on the block party, the event easily turns into a progressive garage party.

Tips
- Solicit donations from guests, their friends and relatives, and local merchants.
- Distribute a "what we'll loan/give/do/find/pay for" volunteer sheet as soon as you establish the date. List the possible themes. Request the prompt return of this sheet, with at least one commitment of goods or time from each invited guest.
- Charge enough admission to hire a professional videographer. An amateur will not be able to create a video good enough to star at next year's gathering.
- Send the guests home with instant photos and goody bags of donated items.

Twists
- Plan a "Wedding Bell Blues" block party, in which everyone gets to dress as a member of the wedding: bride, groom, attendants, flower girls, ring bearer, clergy, band, caterer, florist, and one daring guest may even come as the cake. Organize the party to resemble a wedding reception, with all of the traditional activities being exaggerated and satirized. Have couples bring their wedding photos, and stage a "match couple to photo" contest.
- Whatever theme you use, plan crazy competitions such as Best Decorated Cowboy Hat, Wildest Hawaiian Print, Most Obnoxious Bermuda Shorts, Tackiest Tie, and so on. The fashion show of those vying for titles will be a major source of entertainment.
- Crown a king and queen "of the block": Have guests make nominations before the day of the event. Then at the event, judge the nominees on a talent they've never performed before, on smartness at answering ridiculous trivia questions, and on poise shown while balancing noodles on their noses and other such dignified activities. Crown the king and queen with pomp and ceremony á la Miss America as a hilarious party finale.

For other themes appropriate for your occasion, see the theme grid on page 188.

Part Two
HOLIDAYS

A holiday provides one of the most popular reasons to have a party, because traditional holidays have established, easy-to-follow themes. This section will cover both traditional American and other ethnic holidays, touching upon each holiday's traditions. For those of you who want to add a new twist to your party, each party plan provides some different ideas—some a bit daring—for you to explore.

An example of putting a new twist on a Christmas festivity is to celebrate it with a different theme. You could have a Holiday Hoedown, a Christmas Luau, or a Christmas Down-Under. An exotic theme not only adds excitement and fun to your gatherings, but it also gives your family a chance to learn about life in other parts of the country or the world by trying the food, decorations, costumes, and traditions.

You'll also find ideas for national holidays, those not normally observed with a festive celebration (such as President's Day and Columbus Day), even though these holidays are excellent times to throw a party—to unwind and get together with friends, family, or workmates.

The holiday section will also furnish you with ideas you can use for parties any time of the year, such as a Christmas in July party, a Mardi Gras New Year's Eve party, or a St. Patrick's Birthday Party in August. One of the loveliest weddings I have ever seen followed a Christmas theme, because it was the time of year when the bride and groom first met.

To make this section extra complete, you will find two plans for holidays that only occur every two and half and every four years—Leap Year and Once in a Blue Moon. These unique themes will be a boon to any host who wants to start a tradition without getting committed to an annual event.

NEW YEAR'S DAY

New Year's Day festivities are usually centered around watching the Rose Bowl Parade and game while resting up after a gala New Year's Eve. For many people, New Year's Day traditions are associated with luck and good fortune—specifically, predictions for all the good things to come in the new year. Such traditions make an excellent theme for your party.

Invitation Ideas
- Copy a January calendar page, write the party information with colored ink in the first-day-of-the-month box, and decorate that box with stickers and glitter.
- Make envelopes out of copies of the same page.
- Mail invitations with resolution slips to be filled out and used for admission.

Dress Options
- Casual clothing
- T-shirts or shirts inscribed with resolutions
- Outfits of football game spectators

Decor
- Replicas of good-luck symbols: four-leaf clovers, rabbits' feet, horseshoes, lucky pennies, winning poker hands, completed bingo cards
- Good-luck packages hanging on a Christmas tree (if applicable) or scattered around the party room. These packages could contain various trinkets, and the "lucky" ones could have money.
- For a football crowd: artificial or real roses arranged in vases, around lamp bases, and woven into a garland and draped over the television set; football posters, uniform gear, and signs

Activities
- Read tarot cards, palms, handwriting, tea leaves, numerology.
- Read the resolutions guests brought with them (make some up, if you want), and have guests try to guess who wrote each one.
- For a football crowd: Set up a wager pool and award prize money.
- Play football trivia.
- Have guests who are not football fans produce and perform a halftime show.

Refreshments
- Either a before-game brunch or a hearty buffet lunch, with munch-along snacks stationed within reach
- Ball game beverages: beer, wine, soda, juices, and water

Prizes/Favors
- Salt shakers filled from a fresh box of salt for good luck
- Calendars
- Computerized tarot readings, horoscopes

For other themes appropriate for your occasion, see the theme grid on page 192.

MARTIN LUTHER KING, JR. DAY

This holiday is all about dreams—it celebrates the birth of the man who had dreams of a peaceful and nonprejudiced society. On the third Monday in January, gather to pay tribute to the progress we have made and to share ideas and plans for making all of King's dreams come true.

Invitation Ideas
- Make greeting-card-style invitations; print King's dream speech on the cover and party information on the inside.
- Include a sheet of paper for guests to list their dreams and goals; have them bring the sheet to the party to share with other guests.
- Send the invitations in envelopes made from photocopies of Dr. King's portrait.

Dress Options
- All-black or all-white clothing, with one item to share (accessories and outer garments work well: gloves, scarves, large belts, ties, hats, jackets, cardigans)

Decor
- Photo blowups of the march, of King, and of his speech
- Posters or large sheets of paper on which guests will list important changes made since King's death
- Photo blowups of blacks and whites together in peace

Activities
- Have the guests exchange their extra garment: guests dressed in all black give clothing items to guests dressed in all white.
- Separate guests into teams and have team members take turns giving song, book, or movie titles with the words "black" or "white" in them, replacing the color in the title with "King" (for example: King Beauty, King Christmas, Snow King, and so on). Each title must be recognized by the other team to qualify. The team that runs out of entries first loses.
- Sing "Abraham, Martin, and John," "We Shall Overcome," and "Ebony and Ivory."

Refreshments
- A menu of host's choice, featuring some African delicacies

Prizes/Favors
- Dr. Martin Luther King, Jr. photos, books, or tapes
- Black-and-white stationery items

For other themes appropriate for your occasion, see the theme grid on page 192.

CHINESE NEW YEAR

This festivity begins on the first full moon after January 21 and lasts for fifteen days. That's my kind of celebration! You can have your Chinese New Year party on any of those days.

Invitation Ideas
- Tuck the invitations into fortune cookies; mail in small cartons.
- Print the party details on bright red paper with gold lettering.
- Along with the invitations, send paper and instructions for an origami project.
- Wrap the invitations around pairs of chopsticks; mail in padded envelopes.

Dress Options
- Red, black, and gold casual wear
- Garments with mandarin collars
- Quilted jackets and matching pants

Decor
- Paper lanterns, folding screens
- Decorative fans, bamboo wall coverings, Chinese straw hats
- Red or black satin drapes and table covers
- Travel posters and maps of China, Chinese calendars
- Gold-sprayed take-out cartons filled with poppy flowers and greens, accented with black-lacquered chopsticks and small folding fans, set on lacquered platforms or mirrored trays
- Ornately decorated tea sets
- Embroidered satin wall hangings or table runners

Activities
- Organize tea-leaf readings.
- Play Chinese checkers.
- Play a Charlie Chan Mystery game.
- Teach the guests to eat with chopsticks.

Refreshments
- Chinese feast, either homemade or take-out
- Fresh oranges, the sign of good luck

Prizes/Favors
- Small folding fans on magnets
- Horoscope fortune cookies (See Resources, #23.)
- Chinese cookbooks or cooking utensils
- Coupons for eat-in or take-out Chinese restaurants
- Lacquered chopsticks

For other themes appropriate for your occasion, see the theme grid on page 192.

VALENTINE'S DAY

February 14 pays tribute to St. Valentine, who wrote a tragic love letter to his sweetheart on the day of his death. In the past, you would acknowledge lovers or mates on this day, but now you can find a greeting card that expresses sentiments even to your meter reader or shoe repair person. It's a no-greetings-barred holiday that encourages the unrestrained display of affection—to anyone or anything (in case you have an especially endearing cactus plant).

Trends
- The official colors for Valentine's Day are red, pink, and white. On this day, lace-trimmed, heart-shaped cards, candy, flowers, and sentimental gifts are purchased by the ton. Valentine's Day is an occasion for romantic dinners, marriage proposals, and even weddings.
- Schools, from preschool onward, promote swapping valentine cards and celebrating with parlor games and refreshments.
- Valentine's Day is very popular for fund-raising events, sweetheart dances, theme parties, and restaurant/nightclub promotions.

Tips
- Organize a valentine party to include ice skating or a hay/sleigh ride (in cold-weather areas). Guests will work up an appetite for piping-hot food, such as spicy chili, and steamy beverages, such as cocoa, coffee, mulled cider, and toddies.
- Serve a Valentine's Day menu of red-and-white foods. These can include pasta and tomato sauce, cherry Jell-O with marshmallows, vanilla ice cream with strawberries, milk or fruit juice for the kids, and red or white wine for the grownups.
- Play Valentine's Day trivia games: "Famous Lovers" (kids will know Aladdin and Princess Jasmine, Cinderella and Prince Charming, and so on) or "Heart-Filled" (every answer must have the word "heart" in it: [vegetable] _____ hearts, [movie] _____ Heart, [saying] Getting to the heart of the _____).
- Organize a craft party and have your guests make valentines for family, friends, and classmates.

Twists
- Throw a roaring twenties, prohibition-style costume party. Have your guests dress as flappers and dappers, and as they arrive, inspect them through a peep hole and have them give you the secret password. At the party, dance the Charleston and drink bathtub gin (or ginger ale). (See Roaring Twenties party, page 106.)
- Make a Valentine's Day party plan using the letter V as a theme. For example, Velveeta cheese, veggies, vanilla wafers, vino, and vodka for refreshments; velvet, veils, voodoo dolls, vases, vines, and violets for decor; Viennese waltz, volleyball, videos, ventriloquists for activities. The choices are vast and varied, and the results are victorious. Open the dictionary to V, and let the fun begin.

MARDI GRAS

Mardi Gras is French for Fat Tuesday and is the day before Ash Wednesday: the beginning of Lent, forty days before Easter. It is celebrated in New Orleans with parades, street festivals, and twenty-four-hour-a-day music. People travel from all over the world to attend this wild and wonderful party.

Invitation Ideas
- Attach the invitations to elegantly decorated masks.
- Along with each invitation, send a plain half-mask for each guest to decorate.
- Include trinkets and coins in each envelope.

Dress Options
- Any costume, as long as it is worn with a mask

Decor
- Gold, green, and purple colors
- Balloons, streamers, confetti
- Street signs and street lamps from prop houses
- Posters and paintings depicting Mardi Gras locale and themes
- Ornate masks
- Costume jewelry, crowns, scepters, capes, and other royal trappings
- Musical instruments and other decorations with a music theme

Activities
- Attend a jazz band concert or any other open-air band performance.
- Stage or attend a grand parade.
- Crown best-costume winners to reign as royalty during the party.
- Organize food- and wine-tasting contests.

Refreshments
- Shrimp creole
- Jambalaya
- Rice
- Orange-coconut ambrosia
- French bread
- Pecan pie
- Festive drinks, champagne, and New Orleans specials, such as New Orleans Gin Fizz, New Orleans Punch (See Resources, #48.)

Prizes/Favors
- Trinkets traditionally tossed about at the Mardi Gras Parade: costume jewelry, lace lingerie, silk scarves, and candy
- Chocolate coins in small treasure chests
- Instant photos of costumed guests

For other themes appropriate for your occasion, see the theme grid on page 192.

PRESIDENT'S DAY

The third Monday of February honors all American presidents, especially George Washington and Abraham Lincoln, who previously had separate holidays. If your guest of honor has a birthday or anniversary on this day, elect to base your party around the "famous" birthdays.

Invitation Ideas
- Make color copies of a one and a five dollar bill. Cut out the face and replace with a piece of Mylar paper. Write the message "Cash in on President's Day."
- Write the party details using such phrases as "honest," "cannot tell a lie," and "ask not."
- Send the invitations in white envelopes with red and blue trim.

Dress Options
- Red, white, and blue clothing
- As a president or a president's wife

Decor
- Presidential memorabilia, photos of all presidents mounted on flag paper
- Red, white, and blue bunting
- An enlarged photograph of the White House attached to the front door, and 1600 Pennsylvania Avenue address posted on the mailbox, near the doorbell, or wherever it will be most visible to guests
- Election posters and presidential souvenirs displayed around the room
- An oval-room backdrop behind a big desk, for a serving station
- Hatchet, cherries, three-corner hat and/or stove-pipe hat and old law books

Activities
- Play a Presidential Trivia game.
- Play the Dictionary Game, in honor of George Washington's famous quote: "I cannot tell a lie." (See Party How-To's, #13.)
- Stage a patriotic sing-along (for example: "It's a Grand Old Flag," "God Bless America," "America, the Beautiful," and so on).
- Provide photographs of all the presidents and play Name the President—give Lincoln pennies and one dollar bills for correct answers (when money runs, out winners take from each other).

Refreshments
- A buffet with foods labeled From Abe's Deli, George's Gorgeous Cherry Pie, Teddy's Big Veggie Sticks, Jimmy's Peanut Butter, Ronald's Matinee Popcorn, Franks á la Roosevelt and Benjamin, Anheuser and Bush's Beer, and more

Prizes/Favors
- White House souvenirs
- Banks in the shape of coin
- President baseball cards

For other themes appropriate for your occasion, see the theme grid on page 192.   **45**

LEAP YEAR

Every four years, on February 29, an extra day is added to the month to bring the calendar in line with the earth's orbital clock. Traditionally, on this day all women have a perfect right to make proposals, so bachelors beware and think before you give 'yes' for an answer.

Invitation Ideas
- Make formal wedding invitations, leaving a fill-in-the-blank for the groom's name. As part of the party information, instruct each female to bring two single males (to make the odds more desirable for the women), and instruct the males to wear their running shoes.

Dress Options
- Bridal wear for ladies, in anticipation of the best results
- Leisure wear or formal wear for gentlemen, to indicate if they are determined to remain unmarried or if they are marriage material, respectively

Note: Be sure you have one justice-of-the-peace impersonator.

Decor
- An altar decorated for a wedding ceremony, with flowers, tulle netting, candles, and a hitching post, just in case some guy changes his mind midceremony
- Seating for guests, with an aisle between the chairs
- A barricade, set up after the bride and groom reach the altar; again, to prevent groom getaways
- Crime-scene tape around the altar area
- Honeymoon travel posters, wedding-related artwork, and photos

Activities
- Organize ongoing proposals and ceremonies.
- Have a wedding dance.
- Designate one guest to act as the official wedding photographer (or hire a professional photographer for the party).
- Award a prize to the bride with the most grooms.
- Open gag wedding gifts (each bride should bring a gift to exchange).
- Play a lively game of Wedding Trivia.

Refreshments
- Standard wedding-reception fare: cake, finger sandwiches, mints, nuts, punch, and coffee (Beware of brides spiking punch with "agreeable tonics.")

Prizes/Favors
- Gift certificates for placing personal ads
- How-to books for singles
- Little black books

For other themes appropriate for your occasion, see the theme grid on page 192.

ST. PATRICK'S DAY

St. Patrick's Day, celebrated on March 17, commemorates the patron saint of Ireland, Bishop Patrick, who, in 432 A.D., left his home in the Severn Valley, England, and introduced Christianity into Ireland. The Irish celebrate this holiday with festive parades and gala parties, lively with tall tales, traditional songs, authentic foods, and free-flowing green beer.

Invitation Ideas
- Paint party details on fake or real stones, and send them in padded envelopes.
- Tuck invitations inside green party hats.
- Write party information with green ink on white paper, and trim the invitations with shamrock confetti.
- Enclose name tags with the invitations, and write "Mc" or "O" before each guest's surname.

Dress Options
- Wearin' of the green—of guests' choices

Decor
- Balloons, streamers, banners
- Irish travel posters, maps
- Movie or Broadway show posters of Irish-related shows (*Finian's Rainbow*)
- Giant cardboard cut-outs of theme-appropriate items: shamrocks, leprechauns
- Shamrock plants (live or imitation)
- Lace tablecloths, with potatoes and cabbage as table centerpieces

Activities
- Organize Irish sing-alongs (for example: "When Irish Eyes Are Smiling," "Too-ra, Oo-ra, Loo-ra," and "Danny Boy").
- Name songs with the word "green" in the title.
- Stage a Mr. Potato Head tournament.
- Have a Find-the-Shamrock contest.
- Tell tall tales.
- Put on a parade of Irish costumes or hats.

Refreshments
- Corned beef and cabbage
- Baked-potato bar
- Irish whiskey and Guinness stout
- Irish soda bread
- Irish coffee
- Green ice cream

Prizes/Favors
- Bars of Irish Spring soap
- Color copies of dollar bills, pinned to lapels (for "green")
- Irish-coffee mugs
- "Irish for a Day" buttons
- Shamrock plants

For other themes appropriate for your occasion, see the theme grid on page 192.

EASTER

Easter is a festival celebrated by the Christian Church to commemorate the Resurrection of Christ. This holiday takes place on the first Sunday following the full moon that occurs on or after March 21 (the Vernal Equinox, when the hours of day and night are equal). The week after Easter is called Egg Salad Week, and is dedicated to the many delicious uses for leftover Easter Eggs.

Trends
- Family and friends gather for a hearty Sunday brunch at someone's home or at a family restaurant. Sometimes this celebration involves gift giving. It almost always includes such activities as hunting for festive treat-filled baskets, dyeing and decorating eggs, and playing croquet, volleyball, or softball.

Tips
- Let the older children (nonbelievers in the E. B. [Easter Bunny]) hide eggs, candy, and toys for the tots. Then, while the little ones enjoy their finds, send the big kids on a hunt for plastic eggs filled with coins.
- Organize the kids (young and old) for a challenging game of Pin the Fluffy Tail on the Bunny. Hand draw the bunny on craft paper, and use double-sided tape to attach the cotton-ball tail.
- Lay out a supply of craft items for a Decorate-a-Bonnet project. Produce a lively and fashionable Easter Parade, and award a prize to the winner of the Hippity Hippest Hat contest. Present guests with instant photos of themselves in their crafty and creative chapeaux.
- Be sure to include the popular favorite—everybody-does-it—Bunny Hop!

Twists
- Research another country's Easter customs, and incorporate them into your celebration. For example, serve a meal that introduces your family to another country's food traditions.
- Have elder family members tell stories of their childhood Easter memories. Videotape the stories to make a priceless and treasured documentary to be shown for many future years.
- Dig out old photos of family members wearing hats. Number the photos, line them up on the wall or table, and have the guests identify as many as they can. Give a fun hat, cap, or visor to the person who identifies the most photos.
- Create a new holiday tradition that will give both adults and children an experience of great value: Prepare baskets of treats, deliver them to a nearby retirement home, and hand them out to residents who do not have visitors on Easter. If your group is musically inclined, give a concert of Easter songs.

APRIL FOOLS' DAY

April 1 is the silliest day of the year, awaited with eagerness by all those mischievous imps who enjoy playing jokes and pranks on their friends and relatives. There's fun and games, trickery, and foolery for those brave enough to attend.

Invitation Ideas
- Make greeting-card-style invitations and glue them closed. Write "You are invited to a party" on the front, and add party details on the back.
- Mail the invitations in mailing tubes with pop-out gag snakes. (See Resources, #6.)

Dress Options
- Backwards, upside down, inside out, and hopelessly goofy

Decor
- Everything upside down or sideways
- Silly signs like "Restrooms Upstairs" in a one-story house, "Fresh Paint," and "Out of Order," with missspelled woords (like that)
- Tricks and gags placed around the party room, such as whoopee cushions and sticky doorknobs
- Tablecloths made out of funny papers
- Giant clown shoes (see Resources, #27), big floppy hats, and mislabeled boxes used to serve snacks

Activities
- Put on a Parade of Fools Fashion Show, and give out such bogus prizes as expired show tickets, mismatched socks or gloves, or big rocks in boxes that once held expensive items.
- Have a sing-along of "Foolish" and "April" songs (for example: "Fools Rush In," "Why Do Fools Fall in Love?," "What Kind of Fool Am I?," and "April Showers").
- Show blooper videos.
- Stage a fake stickup or blackout.
- Hire an actor to act as a clumsy waitperson or an eccentric guest.
- Hand out mismatched name tags to the guests, and have them find the corresponding person.

Refreshments
- Funny foods like corn dogs, beef jerky, slushies, s'mores, upside-down cake, Fiddle Faddle (caramel-corn snack), Ding Dongs
- Some luscious-looking "fake" desserts, glued to a plate
- Drinks served in dribble glasses

Prizes/Favors
- Only gag, trick, or useless items
- One nice prize awarded for an activity—and taken back as an April Fools' joke

For other themes appropriate for your occasion, see the theme grid on page 192.

EARTH DAY

Earth day, April 22, was first observed in 1970 to remind us to handle our planet with care. Some observe this day on the vernal equinox. Each component of an Earth Day party must be ecological—you can even recycle the ideas at an "edutainment" family party.

Invitation Ideas
- Print the party details on paper that has already been used on one side. Send the invitations in brown paper bags.

Dress Options
- In any colors of nature, especially green
- Secondhand (recycled) clothing
- Accessories (hats, vests, belts) made out of paper (crush brown paper bags to soften them)

Decor
- Globes and maps
- Trees, bushes, and plants
- Decorations made out of egg cartons, milk cartons, newspapers, magazines, strings, tissue boxes, old nylons, tin cans, plastic bottles, paper rolls, and fabrics (See Resources, #47.)

Activities
- Organize an arts-and-crafts workshop to create gifts for May Day or Mother's Day.
- Have contests: Making the Best Hat, Making the Best Jewelry, Writing the Best Earth Day Poem or Song.
- Play an Earth/world trivia contest.
- Walk or race on stilts made of tin cans and string. (See Resources, #54.)

Refreshments
- Because Earth Day is also Arbor Day, the day Johnny Appleseed is honored, the menu can feature apples in all kinds of recipes, from salads to desserts
- Leftovers casserole and home-baked rolls
- Homemade cider or lemonade

Prizes/Favors
- Seedlings
- Copies of recycling tips and suggestions
- Printed instructions for recycling crafts
- Party Cracker Favors (See Party How-To's, #16.)

CINCO DE MAYO

May Fifth is a Mexican national holiday, celebrated with dancing, music, and food, food, food. Mexicans eat five meals a day, and when you celebrate with them, you are invited to all five.

Invitation Ideas
- Along with the invitations, send tissue paper and instructions to create a flower for señoras or señoritas to wear. (See Party How-To's, #10.)
- Wrap the invitations in brightly colored tissue strips, and send them in tubes.
- Record an RSVP voice-mail message to a background of mariachi music. (See Party Tips, #2.)

Dress Options
- All-white clothing, accented with colorful shawls, flowers, and jewelry
- Authentic Mexican attire: sombreros, serapes (long, blanket-like shawls), and huarache (low-heeled, leather) sandals

Decor
- Mexican flags
- Brilliantly colored paper flowers, balloons, streamers
- Travel posters
- Props such as burros, bales of straw
- Souvenir-type booth for food and beverages
- Piñatas and Mexican paper lanterns, or strings of lights in the shape of sombreros, chili peppers, and cacti
- Luminaria lights on walkways, tables, around pool (See Party How-To's, #9.)

Activities
- Teach a crash course in the Mexican hat dance.
- Set up a make-your-own Mexican meal at grazing stations.
- Make piñatas, then break them open.
- Play guitar music for dancing and listening, and have the audience join in with maracas and percussion instruments.
- Hire a face painter to decorate guests with mustaches, side burns, and flower tattoos.

Refreshments
- Mexican fiesta favorites, such as burritos (tortillas filled with beans and meat), tacos (fried tortillas, folded and filled with meat, shredded lettuce, tomatoes, onions, and salsa), chips and salsa, margaritas, and Mexican beer

Prizes/Favors
- Minisombreros on key chains
- Instant photos of guests in costume
- Lace handkerchiefs
- Baskets of piñata prizes

For other themes appropriate for your occasion, see the theme grid on page 192.

MOTHER'S DAY

This annual day for honoring mothers and motherhood is observed on the second Sunday of May. On this day we show love and appreciation to all the moms in our lives. Mother's Day brunches draw record crowds, and backyard barbecues work overtime at family gatherings. Maybe this is the year you try something different.

Invitation Ideas
- Send attractively packaged tea bags and invitations to an "Our Mom Suits Us to a Tea" party.
- Instruct guests to write a poem or a message about Mom to bring to the party.

Dress Options
- Tea-party outfits for girls: flowered hats, gloves, and so on
- Sunday best for boys
- Vintage, Victorian styles
- As a character out of the *Alice in Wonderland* tea party

Decor
- Old photos of Mom
- Magazine photos of Mom's favorite activities, hobbies, or products—all mounted on doilies, lace paper, or tissue
- Flowers in teapots or cups
- Travel posters of England or of other European views
- Posters from the Tea Association (See Resources, #13.)
- Lace tablecloths, with ribbons and streamers for runners
- Thrift store creamers and tiny pitchers for children's personal teapots

Activities
- Play croquet, horseshoes, checkers.
- Set up a craft table for tissue-paper flower lessons. (See Party How-To's, #10.)
- Present poems and gifts to Mom.
- Have children sing a few choruses of "I'm a Little Teapot."
- Play Pin the Handle on the Teapot.
- Organize tea dancing to recorded music.

Refreshments
- Assorted finger sandwiches
- Fresh berries with whipping cream
- A variety of teas
- Assorted pastries and tarts
- Champagne or fruit punch

Prizes/Favors
- Tea-bag collections
- Instant photos with Mom
- Fun teapots

Note: Another idea for Mother's Day is a "Come as Your Favorite TV Mom" party.

For other themes appropriate for your occasion, see the theme grid on page 192.

MEMORIAL/VETERANS DAY

Memorial Day, formerly called Decoration Day, is celebrated the last Monday in May, in honor of armed forces personnel killed in war. First celebrated in 1868, this holiday. Veterans Day, November 11, commemorates the 1918 ending of World War I and honors the members of the armed forces. These two holidays can be celebrated in almost identical ways.

Invitation Ideas
- Decorate the invitations with red, white, and blue trim, poppies, and flags

Dress Options
- Casual dress
- Military uniforms

Decor
- Red, white, and blue decorations
- Worktable with craft supplies for guests to create holiday hats

Activities
- Have a picnic or a backyard barbecue.
- Play family activities, such as volleyball, softball, touch football, horseshoes, Frisbee, and basketball.
- Ask each guest to bring a holiday-based trivia question. Award a prize to the guest whose question stumps the crowd and to the guest who answers the most questions.
- Display arts-and-crafts results in a wacky fashion show. Give out prizes according to the loudest audience response.
- Organize teams by color for the Official Red, White, and Blue Olympics; be sure to mix children evenly with adults. Run the traditional events: sack race, three-legged race, relay race, tug of war tournament, bag of clothes relay race (teams have to put on the clothes that are in the bag, run to their teammate, undress, and replace clothing into the bag for the next teammate to do the same).
- Create a tape of race music, including "Chariots of Fire," "Rocky's Theme," and "William Tell Overture," to add drama and excitement to the races and to the grand finale awards ceremony.
- Present Olympic medals in a silly ceremony, playing the spoof national anthem of the winning team: "Red River Valley," "Blue Velvet," and "White Christmas."

Refreshments
- Potluck of red, white, or blue foods and beverages (See Party Tactics, page 154.)

Prizes/Favors
- Silk-poppy-flower magnets
- Cassettes or CDs of World War I big-band favorites
- Medals or ribbons
- War books and games
- Videos of famous war episodes

For other themes appropriate for your occasion, see the theme grid on page 192.

FATHER'S DAY

Families gather on the third Sunday in June to pamper Papa with their presence and presents. This day was first celebrated in Spokane, Washington, in 1910, and became a national holiday in 1966.

Invitation Ideas
- Write the party information on pieces of garishly printed gift paper, cut into the shape of a necktie, or attach printed tags to thrift-shop neckties. Request that guests bring Dad totally useless gifts in addition to their "real" gifts.

Dress Options
- Casual attire for relaxation and activity
- As "dear old dad" in his typical leisure-time garb, such as wild-plaid shorts, sweats, robe, and slippers
- Cardboard crown, garishly decorated with glitter, rhinestones, and so on, for Dad

Decor
- Photos of Dad (mounted on colored paper) displayed as in an art gallery
- A clothesline backdrop of Dad's favorite, least-attractive garments, with Dad's favorite seat, lounge chair, hassock, or throne (even that one!) in front of the backdrop—to be used for a formal gift presentation ceremony
- Posters of Dad's favorite movies, television programs, products, or travel destinations

Activities
- Open Dad's gag and serious gifts.
- Tell classic funny, sentimental, or fictional Dad stories.
- Make a "Let's Hear It for Dad" videotape starring all your guests. Watching this tape can be a great way to end the day's activities.

Refreshments
- Hero sandwiches (to further honor Dad)
- Dad's Root Beer (if this brand is available in your area)
- Any of Dad's other favorite foods and beverages

Prizes/Favors
- Instant photos with Dad wearing his crown
- Gift certificates for sandwiches
- Garish neckties

For other themes appropriate for your occasion, see the theme grid on page 192.

FOURTH OF JULY

It's America's birthday, so invite your family, neighbors, class, or club to a party filled with patriotic and participatory fun. Since July is national Hot Dogs, Ice Cream, and Picnics month, use all three themes when planning your party.

Invitation Ideas
- Roll the invitations inside miniflags, and mail them in red fireworks tubes. (See Resources, # 29.)
- Write party information on bandannas with stars-and-stripes designs (or send such a bandanna along with each invitation).

Dress Options
- Uncle Sam and/or colonial costumes for history and costume enthusiasts
- Casual red, white, and blue clothing

Decor
- Balloons, streamers, flags, banners, and posters following the patriotic colors and themes
- Red-and-white checked or striped tablecloths
- Store-bought or hand-crafted table accessories with a stars-and-stripes theme
- Red, white, and blue table and serving ware
- Red or red-and-white decorations recycled from Christmas or Valentine's Day, with added white and blue touches

Activities
- Play name-tag trivia games. (See Party Tips, #4, 7.)
- Parade to a recorded marching band.
- Have pie-eating contests.
- Make ice cream.
- Play horseshoes and other competitive picnic games.
- Have guests work individually or in groups to create their very own flags; then have a contest for the most creative, original, interesting, and so on, flags.
- Stage a patriotic song-fest.
- Organize fireworks displays.

Refreshments
- Picnic fare: burgers, hot dogs, fried chicken, potato salad, coleslaw, baked beans, biscuits
- Home-baked apple pie, homemade ice cream, and freshly squeezed lemonade

Prizes/Favors
- Patriotic souvenirs: postcards, pens, pencils, magnets, sunglasses, bandannas, and scarves

For other themes appropriate for your occasion, see the theme grid on page 192.

BASTILLE DAY

Viva la France! and everything that is representative of the country famous for romance, art, and fine foods. On July 14, messieurs and mademoiselles celebrate the anniversary of the end of the French Revolution with a gala festivity.

Invitation Ideas
- Attach a color photocopy of a well-known painting to the front of each invitation, and frame it with gold trim or paint. Write the party information in familiar French phrases.
- Trim the envelope with red, white, and blue ribbons.

Dress Options
- Peasant costumes of the revolution era
- The "streets of Paris" mode: Apache (a Parisian thug), gendarme, cancan dancer
- Fifi, the French maid, or Pierre, the chef

Decor
- Red-and-white checked tablecloths
- Tables arranged as in a sidewalk café
- Street lights (fake or drawings), umbrellas, trees with twinkle lights
- Candles in wine bottles
- Posters of art, travel locations, products (perfume, fashion, food)
- Mockup of Eiffel Tower
- French flags and banners

Activities
- Organize contests of drawing, crafts, and cooking.
- Have a wine tasting. (See Party Tactics, page 159.)
- Set up an easel, paper, brushes, and paint, and have the guests work together to create one masterpiece. Present it to the host or give it out as a door prize.
- Dance adagios or the cancan.
- Hire entertainment, such as a mime, a magician, or a juggler.
- Arrange to have sketch artists and face painters do their stuff at the party.

Refreshments
- Onion soup
- Fruit and cheese
- Pastries
- Crepes
- Baguettes
- French wines and champagne

Prizes/Favors
- Cookbooks
- Bottles of champagne
- Art pieces (miniature paintings, sculptures, blown glass, and so on)
- Authentic berets
- Perfume samples
- Chest ribbons or medals
- Poster art

For other themes appropriate for your occasion, see the theme grid on page 192.

LABOR DAY

In 1894, Labor Day became a national holiday, honoring labor unions and the worker. On the first Monday in September, people celebrate Labor Day with parades, picnics, and family get-togethers. In addition to celebrating Labor Day, most parents of school-aged children give a few whoops and hollers to show their appreciation for the end of summer.

Invitation Ideas
- Frame the party information with Help Wanted ads, or print the invitations on the backs of time cards.
- Attach tiny tools, paintbrushes, pencils, or other symbols of particular occupations, to the invitations.

Dress Options
- Outdoor active wear
- Uniforms or typical clothing for specific jobs

Decor
- Props representing various occupations and tasks
- Posters and banners promoting employment
- Flags and other red, white, and blue decorations

Activities
- Play Match the Tool to the Job: Hand out a list of various jobs and a list of occupational tools, and have the guests match items from the jobs list with items from the tools list.
- Play the name-tag game: Write names of tools (wrench) on one-half of the name tags, and write scrambled versions of those tools (chrewn) on the other half. Hand out the name tags, and have the guests search for their match. (See Party Tips, #7.)
- Organize outdoor sports and games.
- Assign tasks, such as picking up trash, straightening furniture, and so on. The host gets help, and the guests labor, thus getting into the spirit of the day. Good job!

Refreshments
- Substantial foods for a working crew—served in lunch boxes, brown paper bags, or on cafeteria trays—with such names as Painters' Pot Roast, Truck Drivers' Taters, Electricians' Eggplant, Carpenters' Carrots, and Bakers' Buns
- Beverages with such names as Switchman's Soda, Time Card Punch, and Factory Whistle (one toot, and you're out for the day!)

Prizes/Favors
- Hats, T-shirts, and other gift items saluting laborers

For other themes appropriate for your occasion, see the theme grid on page 192.

COLUMBUS DAY

"In fourteen hundred and ninety-two, Columbus sailed the ocean blue..."—a phrase most of us learned in elementary school, has stayed with most of us. For those of us who are diehard party-goers, Columbus has given us a completely valid reason to celebrate October 12, with a theme based on discovery and/or exploration.

Invitation Ideas
- Write the party details on a map of the original ocean journey.
- Format the party details as a Help Wanted ad, reading: Wanted! Crew members for a four-month ocean cruise leaving Spain August 3 (destination to be announced). Choice of three ships, great meals, adventure, and robust exercise. Contact C. Columbus, c/o Isabella, Queen of Spain.

Dress Options
- Ready to sail the ocean blue
- Authentic period costume

Decor
- Maps, drawings of ships, and sailing paraphernalia
- Travel posters, with flags marking the places passed on the voyage
- Bare plank-board picnic tables, to resemble a shipboard mess

Activities
- Play Columbus' Cruise trivia game.
- Match countries to such cultural contributions as foods, animals, and traditions. For example: Tomatoes were an American contribution to Europe.
- Watch movies of Columbus' voyage (or simply have the movies running on the VCR as background noise).
- Provide Columbus or Isabella costumes, and take pictures of the guests modeling the costumes. (If nothing else, try to find some appropriate hats, and take head shots.)

Refreshments
- Multinational menu: foods from Spain, Italy, Africa, Asia
- Foods and beverages labeled with origins of ingredients

Prizes/Favors
- Instant photos of guests in Columbus or Isabella costumes
- Recipes of menu items served

For other themes appropriate for your occasion, see the theme grid on page 192.

HALLOWEEN

Scary creatures show up on the festival of the dead, the night on which ghosts and dead souls are reputed to make their annual appearance. Although Halloween is officially on October 31, parties often take place on the nearest weekend day or night.

Trends, Tricks, or Treats (Couldn't resist that!)
- Rather than collecting treats from door to door, which started in the 1950s, hosts commonly invite guests to stay inside for a gala time of games, entertainment, and goodies.
- Entertaining children on Halloween is as easy as going shopping! The reason for that? Most of the larger shopping malls throw parties on Halloween, with entertainment, music, refreshments, and even photo sessions for families. Little goblins and ghosts can easily stroll from shop to shop collecting their treats.
- Churches and schools also put on festivities. Community organizations sponsor haunted houses.

Tips
- When planning a costume party, remember to give guests total freedom in the selection or creation of their outfits. (See Party Tactics, page 149.)
- Always take lots of instant photos to use as party favors, and videotape the costumed characters to view at the party or at a future event.
- Throw an easily staged progressive bus party—most bars and restaurants throw costume parties featuring special entertainment, reduced-price drinks, and treats. After the Happy Halloween Hopping, return home for midnight coffins—I mean, coffee and dessert.

Twists
- Plan a treasure hunt at the mall. These hunts need a lot of planning, but they are worth the trouble. (See Party Tactics, page 160.)
- Have a Halloween Hoedown, pardner: horseshoes, hayrides, hamburgers and hot dogs, and maybe even a little hot-licks hooch.
- Or organize your party around another theme: Halloween in Hawaii, Happy Days Halloween, Hootenanny Halloween, Hillbilly Halloween, Hippie Halloween, Hollywood Halloween, and finally, Horror Halloween, which brings us back to the beginning.
- Since Halloween is in October, have an Oktoberfest Beer and Brats Polka Party. Tell your guests to show up as their favorite beer-drinking buddy from movies or television (you will probably get lots of Norms). Arrange for a beer-tasting event. (See Party Tactics, page 159.)

THANKSGIVING

Thanksgiving is celebrated on the fourth Thursday of November. Most families have their set traditions, usually involving the consumption of huge amounts of food, but if you add some new ideas you will ensure your holiday's success. The suggestions below concern special treatment for kids during this traditional family event.

Invitations
- Send thank-you notes to summon your guests to the party.
- Enclose a small, lined sheet of paper for each guest; have the guests make lists of everything they are grateful for, and ask them to bring the lists to the party. (See Activities below.)

Dress Options
- Pilgrim and turkey hats, Indian headdresses, hand-painted plastic bibs—for kids and adults (the kids can make these things during the party as an activity)

Decor
- Kid-sized picnic tables; plastic tablecloths on the floor, picnic-style; or pillows around a coffee table, Japanese style
- Balloons and festive Thanksgiving touches (Pocahontas theme works well)
- Colorful Thanksgiving paper or plastic serving ware, bright tablecloths, or personalized place mats, to emphasize each child's importance

Activities
- Create a video-viewing room and show short (not full-length) sing-along, dance, or movement tapes that kids can follow along.
- Videotape the arrival and activities of youngsters, and give a premier showing as the day's grand finale.
- Have adult(s) dressed in costume read aloud or dramatize a Thanksgiving story.
- Organize some quick 'n' easy craft projects (such as the hats noted in the Dress Options section). You can also have the kids make Christmas gifts or cards.
- Give "What I'm Thankful For" readings during dinnertime: Each person writes his or her message on a slip of paper (adults and older children help preschoolers) and puts it into a hat or bowl. Throughout the dinner, guests take turns reading the messages. As a variation, everyone can leave the messages unsigned, and then guests have to match messages to guests.
- Make Thanksgiving the official "Draw a Name for Christmas" day: Mutually decide the theme for gifts, such as "handmade," "readable," "artwork," "best bargain," "starting with the first letter of the recipient's first name," or "represents a famous person, place, or thing." Set a budget amount. Write the name of everyone present on separate slips of paper, and put them into a hat or bowl. Then have everyone draw a name.

Refreshments
- Minisized portions: Tiny loaves of bread, individual pies, minimolds of Jell-O, turkey breast cut into cookie-cutter shapes (you can use TV trays to serve meals to older children)
- Specialty ice-cream treats

Prizes/Favors
- Craft items the kids made during the evening

Note: Give older children authority and responsibility to oversee planned activities, serve food, and pick up after the younger kids—for cash or a prized gift.

Themes for Thanksgiving Parties
- The Thanksgiving Day Picture Won't Be Complete without You.
  1) Have a family group photo enlarged and made into a jigsaw puzzle.
  2) Along with the invitation, send one puzzle piece to each guest, with instructions to bring the piece to the party.
  3) Complete the puzzle on a piece of poster board.
  4) Write a number in the space of each missing piece. You can designate only a few "prize-winning" numbers, or you can have prizes that correspond to each number (all prizes should be equal in value). If you decide to award prizes for all numbers, mark one or two spaces with a turkey sticker instead of a number. The guests who have the pieces that correspond to the turkey stickers receive special prizes.
  5) Award the prizes.

- Family Film Fest.
  1) Send an invitation reading: "You ought to be in pictures; you ought to be a star. And you will be in the First Annual _____ (family name) Thanksgiving Documentary. Please bring a photo of all family members who are unable to attend."
  2) Recruit a guest as the official videographer to tape a brief interview of each guest. The interview can consist of the guest's name, age, parent's names, and a message entitled "What I'm Thankful For."
  3) Videotape the photos of absent family members and do a voice-over of the absent member's personal information.
  4) Run a premier screening during dessert.
  5) Make copies of the video, and present them as Christmas gifts to each family.

For other themes appropriate for your occasion, see the theme grid on page 192.

HANUKKAH

This festival begins on the twenty-fifth day of the third Hebrew month of Kislev (early December) and lasts eight days. Hanukkah celebrates the Jewish victory over the Syrians in 65 B.C. As the Temple was rededicated, a small amount of sacred oil remained for the holy flame—enough for only one day. Miraculously, the oil burned for eight days. Hence, Hanukkah is also called the Miracle (and also, Festival) of Lights.

Trends
- Traditionally, families celebrate joy, religious freedom, and faith. The central symbol of Hanukkah is the menorah, a candleholder that holds nine candles— one candle for each day of Hanukkah, and a ninth, called the shammash, that is used to light the others. On the first night of Hanukkah, one candle is lit; the next night two are lit; and so on for eight days.
- The menorah is placed prominently in a window, so its light can greet guests and announce its owners' feelings of pride in their heritage.
- The decor is subtle and symbolic; colors are royal blue, white, and silver.
- Potato latkes with applesauce and sour cream are the traditional food; "latke" is the Yiddish word for "pancake."
- Hanukkah is a time for songs, stories, games, riddles, prayers, and food. A popular children's game is spinning the dreidel (a traditional spinning toy) for pennies, candy coins, trinkets, or points that go toward the "championship" award.
- Parents usually give each child a small, but significant, gift for each night, and then give a special gift on the last night.

Tips
- Make invitations in the shape of the Star of David, a menorah, or a dreidel.
- Give Hanukkah gelt (money) to children; use real or gold-wrapped-chocolate coins.
- Exchange gifts among children and adults. For large groups, have members draw the name of one person to whom they will give a gift.
- Be sure to make special preparations for the children, such as special seating (make seating cards using tiny bags of candy labeled with the kids' names), mini-sized foods, and well-organized activities.
- Set up small, blue or white plastic chairs, purchased at a dollar store, for all the kids. Write the child's name and the party's date on the back of each chair, and decorate the chairs with Star of David designs. These chairs make great favors.

Twists
- Organize small card-game tournaments. Start a tradition by selecting a special trophy that will be passed from winner to winner each year.
- Make a family video of interviews, songs, poems, and activities. Each year, show the video from the previous year, for fun and reminiscing.
- Prepare a special welcome gift, poem, or song for nonfamily guests.

For other themes appropriate for your occasion, see the theme grid on page 192.

CHRISTMAS

You can entertain successfully during this hectic time of year when you are busy with shopping, cooking, and attending traditional gatherings and parties. Your own December 25 event may follow family or holiday traditions, it may hold a few surprises, or it can be a total departure from the expected. In addition to event-planning tips, below you will also find some holiday season survival tactics.

Trends
- Potluck events are popular with hosts, because guests share expense and effort.
- An organized bus, car caravan, or limo tour of holiday lights is a fun, atypical celebration. The tour can end with dessert, coffee, and holiday drinks at the host's home, office (if this is an office party), or a rented party room.
- Many people add a charitable feature to their holiday celebrations: Guests bring food items, toys, or gifts for the needy.

Tips
- Plan your party at an off-beat time: Saturday or Sunday brunch, a weekday after-work open house, or a weekday after-dinner dessert. Your guests may be more likely to accept an invitation for a time other than a standard Friday or Saturday night.
- Include a few holiday tasks, such as trimming the tree, addressing cards, wrapping gifts, making craft items, cooking, or baking, as part of your party activities.
- Designate a TV-viewing room for kids. Supply it with its own snack bar, comfy seating (such as pillows on the floor), and show holiday videos.
- Have teenagers take party photos with single-use cameras.
- Plan a separate bar for kids, tended by a teenage or older child. Stock the kids' bar with plenty of napkins, straws, and small, sturdy plastic cups/glasses for each child (write each child's name on his or her glass). Serve soft drinks and juices, and provide garnishes, such as cherries and other fruit, cocktail umbrellas, and silly-shaped ice cubes.
- Organize a gift-making activity for kids. Provide craft supplies needed to make delightful presents for parents, grandparents, or siblings. Be sure to include gift-wrapping supplies.
- Videotape guest interviews and self-introductions. Watch the tapes that day or at a future event, and then save them for posterity. Videotape all events, such as caroling, the light display tour, and crafting.

Note: Recycle Christmas cards. Cut off the inside flap and make a postcard out of the front. It is especially fun to send the card back to its original sender—sort of "many happy returns."

Twists
- Videotape the comic ritual of assembling the toys. If you film the process in various stages of completion, the result can be pretty hilarious—especially if the process seems, as in most cases, impossible.

For other themes appropriate for your occasion, see the theme grid on page 192.

- Plan your holiday party with a theme, such as Holiday Hoedown, International Food Fest, Hawaiian Holiday, Festive Fiesta, Victorian Christmas, Old-Fashioned Country Christmas, Christmas Craft Fair, Cruise Ship Christmas, Caribbean Christmas, Chinese Christmas, or Clam-Bake Christmas—and many more that don't necessarily have to start with a C.
- Plan a tailgating party at the mall to give your guests a shopping break. After shoppin' till they're droppin', your guests can relax, socialize, and enjoy refreshments and music before they head for home. For a luxurious touch, hire masseurs to give guests foot and shoulder massages.
- Organize a caroling party at a nearby retirement home. Take along refreshments, festively wrapped token gifts, and plenty of holiday spirit to give to the residents along with your choral presentation.
- Take instant photos of adult guests sitting on Santa's knee. The guests' children will love to see their parents behave like kids, so the photos make great gifts.

 For other themes appropriate for your occasion, see the theme grid on page 192.

#

Kwanzaa is an African American cultural festival founded in 1966 by Dr. Maulana Karga, a professor at California State University at Long Beach. Kwanzaa is celebrated from December 26 to January 1, and is a time for paying tribute to ancestors. A Kwanzaa feast, called karamu, takes place on the sixth day of the seven-day festival. Kwanzaa is Swahili for "first fruits of the harvest."

Invitation Ideas
- Make the invitations out of colored paper—black, green, and red—possibly woven as a "mkeka" (mat).
- Trim the invitations and envelopes with black, green, and red ribbons.

Dress Options
- Clothing and hats made out of fabrics with traditional Kwanzaa colors and designs

Decor
- Wall drapings and table covers made out of fabrics with Kwanzaa colors and designs
- African artifacts, travel posters, and artworks
- Kinara candleholders
- Black-lacquered baskets filled with fruits and vegetables (especially green and red in color)

Activities
- Create mkeka mats, baskets, and kinara candleholders. (See Resources, #56.)
- Play traditional music, and dance traditional dances.
- Tell stories and discuss the accomplishments of African Americans.
- Light the Kwanzaa candles.
- Make audio or videotapes on which guests introduce themselves to ancestors. Tapes should include guests' important biographical facts, as well as an update of experiences of the past year. This tape, although prepared for ancestors, will be valued by many generations to come.
- Watch movies and read books to explore history and traditions.

Refreshments
- A Kwanzaa feast, or karamu, with fresh corn and a variety of fresh fruit
- Juice shared from a unity cup

Prizes/Favors
- Kwanzaa books for children
- Baskets of nuts painted red and green
- Green and red apples, stems tied with festive ribbons or yarns

For other themes appropriate for your occasion, see the theme grid on page 192.

NEW YEAR'S EVE

On the night of December 31, we are supposed to "let out the old and let in the new." In the pioneer days, people accomplished this by throwing open the windows to shoo out stale, old air and to welcome in fresh, new air. They also celebrated the end of the year by shooting guns on the streets. While gun-shooting is not such a great idea anymore, we do still manage to raise a ruckus with noisemakers, car horns, foghorns, and fireworks.

Trends
- New Year's Eve is traditionally a romantic night for couples. It is a night of proposals, and even elopements. However, singles without dates need not stay home, for it is quite acceptable to attend parties at bars, clubs, and community centers alone. In fact, some elegant affairs are planned for singles only.
- A New Year's Eve celebration often includes the whole family, with game playing, lively competitions, music, and food.
- Gala New Year's Eve parties that benefit charities are popular.

Tips
- Plan your New Year's Eve bash as a costume party, treasure hunt, mystery party, or board game tournament.
- Organize a progressive party, and have your guests stroll, bike, skate, or drive short distances to a series of locations. Each stop should offer a different meal course, activity, or gift, as well as competitions and contests for individuals, couples, or teams. This is great, safe fun that does not end at midnight. Instead, it goes until the wee hours of the morning, with breakfast as a grand finale. A progressive party can be for adults only or can include whole families.

Twists
- Have a Singles-Come-Solo New Year's Eve Party and call it a Last-Chance-for-Romance Dance.
- Plan your party along a Happy Birthday to Everyone! theme. To celebrate the New Year and the event of getting a year older, every guest gets to help blow out candles on a huge cake and open his or her gift (ask each guest to bring a gift to exchange). You can use this simple theme to organize an old-fashioned kids' party: have parlor games; decorate with balloons and crepe paper; and serve such typical party foods as cake, ice cream, and sandwiches. This theme is wonderful for the whole family or for adults only.

For other themes appropriate for your occasion, see the theme grid on page 192.

ONCE IN A BLUE MOON

Every twenty-nine and a half months, two full moons occur in the same calendar month. The second occurrence is called a Blue Moon. So once in a blue moon you have a lovely excuse to gather together with friends for a delicious meal, some music, and a little moon gazing.

Invitation Ideas
- Write the party information with silver ink on blue paper.
- Decorate the invitations with blue ribbons and moon and star shapes made out of Mylar pieces or other shiny confetti.
- Make the envelopes from astrological paper, blue with white lettering. (See Resources, #46.)

Decor
- Blue paper lantern for your blue moon
- Moon-and-stars mobiles
- Blue, gold, and silver decorations and tableware
- Star garlands wrapped around blue candles
- Luminaria bags with star-and-moon cutouts (See Party How-To's, #9.)
- Posters from a planetarium

Activities
- Have a sing-along of "blue" and "moon" songs.
- Gaze at the moon and the stars.
- Play blues music.

Note: Absolutely no mooning!

Refreshments
- Drinks: Blue Curacao, Blue Nun, Blueberry Wine
- Blue ice cubes made by freezing blue water in ice cube trays
- Chicken Cordon Bleu with bleu cheese salad
- Blueberry Jell-O, blueberry cheesecake

Favors/Prizes
- Beautiful things that are either blue or moon-related: soaps, candles, party paper supplies, jewelry, trinkets, and stationery
- Blue minibottles of homemade bleu cheese dressing

For other themes appropriate for your occasion, see the theme grid on page 192.

Part Three
PARTY THEMES

Theme parties are popular because planning them is much more fun and, actually, much easier than planning a party without a theme. A theme is essentially a road map and a menu combined to help you reach your destination and, once there, to make sure that you have everything you need. For example, if you were asked to go into a huge storeroom to select twenty nondescript items, the task would seem unclear. On the other hand, if the request was to gather twenty purple, cloth items typically worn by a woman, the task would become focused.

A theme will focus and pull together the various aspects of a party, thus alleviating a lot of your party-planning anxiety; once you have a "destination," the "what to pack" list will produce itself.

The theme plans in this section will allow you to take your guests on a trip around the world, on a journey back to the past, into the future, and to other places (real or fabricated) they've only imagined. In addition, you will find a wide assortment of themes to use when paying special tribute to a particular person, by basing the party around his or her hobby, interest, pastime, or occupation.

Whether you are planning a party to celebrate a personal milestone, a school or church function, a business-related event, or a whimsical get-together just for fun, this section has a theme plan for you. You can follow the provided themes closely, use only some of the options, or use the suggested ideas with additional details of your own creation.

ATLANTA/DEEP SOUTH

As a tribute to Atlanta or the deep South, plan a party with a theme that follows the classic movie *Gone with the Wind*. You can stage a lavish event with costumes, authentic decor, and a delicious southern repast, or have a less-elaborate party, minimizing or deleting the costumes and decor.

Invitation Ideas
- Create greeting card-style invitations with *Gone with the Wind* poster-replica art on the cover, and party information inside.
- Send a sheet of *Gone with the Wind* trivia questions with the invitations. Guests must bring answers to the party.

Dress Options
- Appropriate costumes from rental shops or local community theater groups
- T-shirts with a line from the movie printed or painted on the front—the more obscure, the better

Decor
- Southern backdrops, movie and travel posters, movie stills
- Sets recreating scenes from the movie (See Party Tips, #6.)
- Handmade or rented accessories (elaborate hats, parasols, and "flutter face" fans)
- Tables covered with lace or floral print cloths
- Peaches, magnolia and cotton blossoms arranged in white wicker baskets trimmed with leaf-green ribbons
- A tribute to Carol Burnett: A take-off on the famous green curtains with yellow fringe draped behind the buffet table or over the entryway

Activities
- Have the guests try to match the T-shirt lines with the movie's characters.
- Act out *Gone with the Wind* scenes for a video documentary.
- View documentary video.
- Watch the movie on a big screen (or just have it playing in the background).

Refreshments
- "Southern-a-fied" menu: southern-fried chicken, black-eyed peas, grits, greens
- Mint Juleps and Southern Comfort whiskey
- Iced teas and coffees, Scarlet O'Hara Cocktails (See Party How-To's, #11.)
- Peaches, fresh or in any recipe

Prizes/Favors
- Silk magnolia flowers
- T-shirts with the Rhett Butler line, "Frankly, my dear,..."
- Southern recipes in a book or booklet
- *Gone with the Wind* memorabilia
- Decorative face fans

For occasions appropriate to this theme, see the theme grid on page 188.

HAWAII/LUAU

A tantalizing, tropical, island get-away party, held indoors or outdoors, is a welcome "trip" at any time of the year. Casual activities and refreshments enjoyed in a languourous, lush, and lazy atmosphere will make your guests' dreams of paradise come true.

Invitation Ideas
- Along with each invitation, enclose a lei and a suntan lotion sample; mail in see-through tubes or envelopes.
- Write a desert island plea for rescue on a scrap of paper; float (mail) in clear bottles. (See Party How-To's, #4.)
- Send the invitations in envelopes made of floral fabric or paper.

Dress Options
- Blindingly bright floral print shirts and shorts
- Sarong/muumuu dresses
- Grass skirts

Decor
- Grass mats, fish netting, palm trees, seashells, floral fabrics, fresh or paper flowers (See Resource, #2.)
- Lanterns or tiki lamps
- "Throne" seat (for the guest of honor)
- Props such as lava fountains, tiki statues, and masks
- Grass hut for treasure and trinket shopping
- Sandy area and beach chairs for sunbathers (If making an indoor beach, cover the floor with a large plastic sheet or a flat bed sheet before spreading the sand.)
- Sun lamps, if possible
- Glass bowls half-filled with water, with live goldfish or fish-shaped candles (See Party Tips, #6.)

Activities
- Organize hula (hoops or dancing) lessons and contests. You may want to contact a local dance school to arrange for inexpensive lessons or an exhibition.
- Lead treasure hunts.
- Have limbo dancing contests.
- Put on a Trim-the-Hat, Sandals, or Sunglasses contest and/or fashion show and give out awards for the most creative design.
- Have a sing-along of Don Ho songs (Don Ho is the best-known singer of the Hawaiian islands).
- Make paper flowers. (See Party How-To's, #10.)
- Play live or recorded steel guitar and ukulele music.
- Write postcards. (See Bon Voyage party, page 30.)

For occasions appropriate to this theme, see the theme grid on page 188.

Refreshments
- Barbecued and deep-fried appetizers
- Fresh fruits and salads
- Steamed veggies
- Glorified rice (a mixture of rice, whipping cream, nuts, bananas, coconut, and other fruit)
- Island beverages (including Hawaiian Punch) served in exotic containers

Prizes/Favors
- Beachcomber hats or flowers for the hair
- Orchids and Hawaiian Ti plants (A Ti plant is a small, wooden block that grows into a plant once it is soaked in water.)
- Shell jewelry or refrigerator magnets
- Macadamia nut delicacies
- Coconut oils and lotions
- Tropical fragrances
- Stamped vacation postcards

For occasions appropriate to this theme, see the theme grid on page 188.

NEW YORK, NEW YOR

Start spreadin' the news that you're having a Big Apple bash. If you plan carefully and completely, your guests can really "be a part of it" and experience the sights, sounds, and smells of New York City—all without having to pack a bag or hop a jet.

Invitation Ideas
- Format your invitation information to look like the front page of the *New York Times*, with a headline announcing the party.
- Roll up the invitations and mail them in plain-paper addressed sleeves.
- Or hand-deliver the invitations for a late-breaking news impact.

Dress Options
- As characters from Broadway Theater, Greenwich Village, or Central Park (count on at least one bag person)

Decor
- Scenes created to depict the above locations
- Ongoing slide presentation of typical New York shots
- Vendors' carts
- Table markers and decor resembling New York's famous restaurants: Russian Tearoom (lace tablecloths), Tavern on the Green (twinkling lights), or Carnegie Deli (checkered tablecloths)
- Theater marquees, playbills, travel posters, event posters, art posters

Activities
- Stage a Broadway show tune songfest (could be a Match-Tune-to-Show game).
- Organize carriage rides, if applicable.
- Dance to music of all styles.
- Eat food from street vendor's carts.
- Appoint (or hire) shell-game skammers and other con artists to amaze and amuse.
- Have an arts-and-crafts show (the guests can be the artists and the customers).

Refreshments
- Coney Island hot dogs, hot pretzels, roasted chestnuts served from a pan
- Deli foods (with sandwiches named after guests)
- Ethnic foods (representing China Town, Little Italy, Little Odessa, and so on)
- Beverages to complement the menu—seltzer to champagne

Prizes/Favors
- Souvenir postcards, T-shirts, hats
- I "heart" Apple items
- Statue of Liberty foam hats (See Resources, #27.)
- Small containers of New York foods

For occasions appropriate to this theme, see the theme grid on page 188.

ARK MOUNTAINS

zarks, somewhere near Dogpatch, when life slowed down to a
he typical hillbilly was often found sitting on his front porch sip-
er" from a little brown jug. This mountain theme is reminiscent of
rkin's Day dances held in high school.

Invitation Ideas
- Tie the invitations around corncobs; send in padded envelopes.
- Write the party information on brown paper bags; send in small muslin bags.
- Record an RSVP voice-mail massage with mountain music in the background.

Dress Options
- Bib overalls, plaid shirts, barefoot or lil' Abner boots, blacked-out teeth
- Mountain ladies' fashions á la Daisy Mae, with pigtails and freckles

Decor
- Front porch atmosphere, with rocking chairs and benches
- Old washing machine, washboard, and a rickety table set up as background for photo opportunities
- Signs misspelled and written backwards
- Oilcloth on tables
- Fruit jars with field flowers and weeds
- Clothesline with laundry, including hole-filled garments, bloomers, and long johns

Activities
- Race barefoot.
- Dance to a washtub-and-washboard mountain band.
- Have a hog calling contest.
- Organize a "Knock the tin can off the shelf with a slingshot" contest (outdoors!).
- Appoint a Marryin' Sam to perform wedding ceremonies. (Furnish a bedraggled bouquet and wedding veil for shotgun brides.)
- Play good old mountain music (live or recorded).
- Have a Hatfields and McCoys tug of war.

Refreshments
- Food served family-style in china crockery, enamelware, and cast-iron pots
- Moonshine from jugs, Mountain Dew, Hills Brothers Coffee
- Porcupine pie (chocolate)

Prizes/Favors
- Fake wedding licenses and rings
- Bandannas or hair ribbons
- Corncob pipes
- Tapes or albums of mountain music

For occasions appropriate to this theme, see the theme grid on page 188.

SOUTHWEST

This theme is chosen not only for its foods, but for its beautiful color scheme. By serving the best foods and displaying decorations associated with the area, you will surely set the atmosphere for a distinctive and delightful party.

Invitation Ideas
- Attach each invitation to a small cactus in a small, terra-cotta pot, trimmed with feathers and ribbons in the Southwestern hues of teal, peach, and mauve.
- Write the party information on cutouts shaped like coyotes or cacti.
- Mail the invitations in envelopes made out of travel magazine pages.

Dress Options
- Dresses, jeans, and western shirts in denim, chambray, or gauze, in pastel colors

Decor
- Strings of lights shaped like cactus plants or chili peppers
- Twinkle lights draped on real cacti
- Statues, photos, stuffed figures, or paintings of road runners or coyotes
- Terra-cotta bowls or pots filled with desert flowers (real, if possible)
- Woven rugs and wall wall hangings
- Southwestern travel and art posters and artifacts
- White-washed oak seating arrangement for photo sessions
- Luminaria bags with coyote and cactus cutouts (See Party How-To's, #9.)
- Candles in candleholders, votive glasses, and standing candelabras
- Linens, china, crockery ware, and table decor in the color theme

Activities
- Have southwestern music and dancing.
- Conduct arts-and-crafts miniclasses: pottery and jewelry making, sand painting.
- Hand out song sheets and stage a sing-along of area-related songs (for example: "Rocky Mountain High," "Down Among the Sheltering Palms," and "By the Time I Get to Phoenix").
- Organize games of horseshoes.

Refreshments
- Southwestern food favorites, such as blue chips and salsa and grilled mesquite foods, served on heavy wooden planks spread across sawhorses
- Beverages with such names as Coyote Cooler and Cactus Cooler

Prizes/Favors
- Tapes or CDs of southwestern music
- Bandannas or scarves in southwestern colors
- Small terra-cotta bric-a-brac and picture frames, cactus plants
- Instant photos of guests in decorative settings

For occasions appropriate to this theme, see the theme grid on page 188.

WEST

Gather all of your little (or big) buckaroos and buckarettes for a way-out West Texas hoedown. It is truly the most popular theme for holidays, special events, and all kinds of occasions. This theme was hot before country was "cool."

Invitation Ideas
- Write the party information on western bandannas, trimmed with toy star badges, rope, bits of hay, or straw.
- Make the envelopes out of craft paper or leather-look paper bags.
- Format the invitations as Outlaw Wanted posters, with mirror-like Mylar in the photo area.

Dress Options
- Cowboy and cowgirl outfits

Decor
- Hay bales and fence rails
- Lamp posts and empty kerosene lamps (See Resources, #27.)
- Cardboard or prop cacti and other dried desert plants
- Strings of party lights (boot- or cactus-shaped)
- Luminaria bags (See Party How-To's, #9.)
- Saddles, bridles, and harnesses draped over sawhorses
- Burlap, denim, or red-and-white checked tablecloths
- Cowboy hats and straw flowers for table centerpieces, with bandanna napkins tied with rope
- Enamelware, crocks, cast-iron pans, baskets, and buckets used as food containers

Activities
- Give country line- and square-dancing lessons.
- Put on a Karaoke Kountry singing contest.
- Organize hay- or pony rides, if possible.
- Have a Trim a Ten-Gallon Hat contest.
- Dance to a western band or to recorded music.
- Have a campfire sing-along.

Refreshments
- Buffet of barbecue favorites
- Sarsaparilla, home-brewed beer, cactus juice
- Chili with cornbread
- Beef jerky

Prizes/Favors
- Good Luck horseshoes, painted gold and lettered with date and occasion
- Barbecue sauces and western snacks
- Bandannas
- Country-western music tapes

For occasions appropriate to this theme, see the theme grid on page 188.

BRITAIN/PUB

When we think of a British theme, we instantly think of the lads from Liverpool—the Beatles! Well, go right ahead and plan your pub party around a Beatles' theme, and your guests will "Love You, Yeah, Yeah, Yeah!"

Invitation Ideas
- Write the party information on a blank record sleeve of a 45 record, and title it "Sergeant [Guest of Honor]'s Lonely Hearts Club Band." (You should be able to find record sleeves at thrift stores; or make them yourself using plain paper.)
- Record an RSVP voice-mail greeting with Beatles' music in the background.
- Superimpose the guest-of-honor's face over a picture of a Beatle's face, then copy and attach it to the invitations.

Dress Options
- Casual, pub-crawling clothing
- Beatles' getups
- Fashions from the Beatles' era

Decor
- English pub atmosphere, with very low lighting and Tiffany lamps
- Game tables
- Wooden bar with bottles lined up on the wall (can be a painted backdrop)
- Beatles' posters, photos, magazine pages, and record album covers
- English travel posters, maps, and flags

Activities
- Play games of darts, pool, checkers, and dominoes.
- Have a Name That Beatles' Tune contest.
- Play Beatles and British Isles trivia games.
- Stage a Beatles Look- and Sing-Alike contest.

Refreshments
- Fish and chips
- Bangers (English sausage)
- Steak and kidney pie
- Tea, cakes, and "ices"
- Wine, beer, and ale by the pint, foot, or yard

Prizes/Favors
- Instant photos of guests standing next to a Beatle look-alike or a life-sized cardboard cutout of a Beatle (See Resources, #1.)
- Royal memorabilia
- Beatles' memorabilia of any kind
- Gag Beatles' wigs

For occasions appropriate to this theme, see the theme grid on page 188.

CARIBBEAN

Treat your guests to a dreamy, tropical experience by planning your party around the scenes, food, and music of the Caribbean Islands. You can either plan a lush, warm, outdoor event, or stage your party indoors during the cold-weather months.

Invitation Ideas
- Tuck each invitation into a travel brochure.
- Write the party information on picture postcards from the Caribbean.
- Along with the invitations, send samples of tropical tanning oil or lotion.

Dress Options
- White linen garments or brightly colored floral prints
- As island natives, in cut-off jeans and bare midriffs
- As island beauties, in off-the-shoulder peasant dresses

Decor
- Palm trees, tropical flowers (real, if possible)
- Lounge chairs with attached drink trays
- Small booth with thatched roof for souvenirs
- Bandstand for reggae band

Activities
- Listen and dance to reggae and calypso music.
- Do the limbo.
- Have a calypso sing-along, and play along on drums and homemade instruments.
- Teach a quick course in making paper flowers. (See Party How-To's, #10.)
- Shop at the Caribbean Kiosk (the one you set up) for travelers' trinkets and treasures.

Refreshments
- Jamaican Jerk
- Chicken and fish entrées, featuring coconut, bananas, and raisins
- Rum drinks, wines
- Jamaican Blue Mountain Coffee

Prizes/Favors
- Island novelties and trinkets
- Packets of Jamaican Blue Mountain Coffee
- Coconut- and raisin-based trail mix
- Tapes and CDs of reggae music

For occasions appropriate to this theme, see the theme grid on page 188.

GERMANY/OKTOBERFEST

Oktoberfest began in October 17, 1810, as a festival celebrating the wedding of King Ludwig I of Bavaria. A festive fall party theme that gives the beer, brats, and kraut crowd a chance to kick up their heels while dancing a lively polka or to just sit back on their heels and enjoy the Oktoberfest show.

Invitation Ideas
- Attach tiny German flags to the invitations, or Bavarian flags, for extra authenticity, (see Resources, #7) and include *Guten Tag!* in your greetings.
- Make greeting-card-style invitations, and attach the map of Europe to the front of each invitation. Glue a tiny flag and ribbon on Germany.
- Send your invitations in aluminum beer cans with decorative product labels—Löwenbräu, if possible. (See Party How-To's, #2.)

Dress Options
- As authentic Herren in lederhosen and Fräuleins in festive dirndl dresses
- Bavarian suits, Alpine hats
- Any clothing in flag colors: black, red, and gold—for Germany; and light blue and white—for Bavaria

Decor
- German and Bavarian travel posters, magazine pictures, flags, and maps
- Roses, the symbol of love (for the wedding celebration)
- Authentic articles of clothing hanging on walls and draped over furniture, safely away from food and beverages
- Giant postcards of tourist spots (See Party How-To's, #7.)

Activities
- Dance to a polka band.
- Have a folk-dancing demonstration.
- Organize beer and wine tasting.
- If held outdoors, play soccer games.
- Have beer-drinking contests. (Be careful about drinking and driving, though!)

Refreshments
- Brats, wurst sausages
- German beer and wine
- German potato salad, potato dumplings
- Pretzels
- Apple strudel
- German chocolate cake

Prizes/Favors
- German beers and wines
- German souvenirs from party catalogs (See Resources, #7.)
- German food delicacies from the supermarket "around the world" section
- Beer mugs or steins

For occasions appropriate to this theme, see the theme grid on page 188. **79**

GREECE

Little compares with the lifestyle enjoyed on a Greek island. By treating your guests to the country's world-famed food, music, and folksy camaraderie, you will transport them to the land where the Olympics originated.

Invitation Ideas
- Write the party information to look like Greek hieroglyphics.
- Attach tiny Greek flags to the invitations.
- Tuck each invitation into a travel brochure.

Dress Options
- Traditional Greek costumes: sailors, folk dancers
- As a tourist

Decor
- Fish netting draped on tables
- Olive branches, tulips, laurel leaves, oleander, hibiscus, jasmine
- Greek columns, small sculptures
- Greek travel posters, artwork, and flags (See Resources, #7.)
- Signs: Tavera (tavern)
- Neon decorations (a Greek invention)

Activities
- Stage mini-Olympics contests.
- Dance and listen to Greek folk music and songs.
- Demonstrate food-preparation techniques.
- Have wine tasting.
- Teach Syrtaki dancing (traditional Greek folk dances).

Refreshments
- Olives and feta cheese appetizers
- Lamb shish kebabs
- Dolma (grape leaves stuffed with rice, lamb, and herbs)
- Ouzo liquor, Retsina wine, coffee
- Grapes
- Baklava

Prizes/Favors
- Greek fishing hats
- Fancy olive oils or olives
- Worry beads

ITALY

An Italian feast is the mainstay of a fabulous Italian theme party. You can create your menu from dozens of pasta dishes, pizzas, salads, and breads that are easy to make and popular with groups of all ages. Whether your guest of honor is of Italian descent, just traveling to Italy, or simply loves Italian food, this theme is *molto bene.*

Invitation Ideas
* Trim the invitations with a few pieces of small pasta and a tiny Italian flag.
* Tie each invitation with a ribbon around two breadsticks and mail in a cardboard tube.
* Tuck each invitation inside a travel brochure.

Dress Options
* All-white clothing

Decor
* Red and green decor
* Italian travel posters, flags, maps
* Cardboard cutouts of the Tower of Pisa, the statue of David, gondoliers (See Resources, #7.)
* Red-and-white checked tablecloths
* Chianti bottles holding candles
* Centerpieces of bread, vegetables, and large pastas

Activities
* Listen to opera or folk music.
* Have an Italian language lesson.
* Play a trivia game: Match Italian notables with claim to fame (for example: Marconi—invented the radio, Francisco Scavullo—photographer, and for laughs, Spaghetti—invented the strap).

Refreshments
* Antipasto
* Pasta, pizza
* Risotto rice
* Salads with vinegar and olive oil dressing
* Gelato (Italian ice cream)
* Cappuccino and espresso coffee

Prizes/Favors
* Breadstick or pasta bouquet
* Coupons for Italian restaurants
* Opera tapes or CDs
* Italian recipe books
* Sauces

For occasions appropriate to this theme, see the theme grid on page 188.

JAPAN

Parties with a Japanese theme are very popular. And considering that the colors of the Japanese flag are red and white, a Japanese-theme party is very apropos during the Christmas holiday season. By adding some green with plants and decorations, the look of the party will be *ichiban* (Japanese for "number one").

Invitation Ideas
- Attach each invitation to a pair of chopsticks.
- Along with each invitation, send a sheet of origami paper and instructions for an origami project.
- Along with each invitation, send a decoratively packaged tea bag.
- Stencil or stamp oriental designs onto wrapping paper, and use that paper to make the envelopes. Write addresses in gold ink.

Dress Options
- Kimonos
- Happi coats and thong sandals

Decor
- Japanese folding screens
- Japanese lanterns or strings of lights
- Japanese travel posters, flags, artwork
- Bonsai plants, flower arrangements
- Hanging displays of kimonos and silk paintings
- Kite and origami displays

Activities
- Share thoughtfully wrapped gifts—the Japanese believe that the wrapping is as important as the gift selection. (See Resources, #51.)
- Organize sumo wrestling: Guests put on inflated suits, and then wrestle. (Find in the *Yellow Pages,* under "carnivals.")
- Listen to Japanese music.
- Act out short plays.

Refreshments
- Tempura, sushi, sashimi, hand rolls—served on low tables with pillow seating
- A variety of teas, especially green tea
- Sake served in authentic sake cups
- Plum wine
- Fruit for dessert

Prizes/Favors
- Decorative fans
- Discount coupons for Japanese restaurants
- Bonsai plants
- Chopsticks

For occasions appropriate to this theme, see the theme grid on page 188.

SWITZERLAND

For those who are "fond of fondue," this cook-it-yourself party theme is ideal. Ski enthusiasts or not, your guests will feel right at home in an atmosphere reminiscent of a Swiss Alpine chalet. Add traditional holiday greens to a decor of red and white, the colors of the Swiss flag, to create a lovely Swiss-flavored Christmas party.

Invitation Ideas
- Tuck each invitation inside a Swiss Alps travel brochure.
- Attach a small piece of Swiss chocolate to each invitation, for a tasty touch.
- Record a voice-mail RSVP message that includes authentic Alpine music, featuring a yodeler. (See Party Tips, #2.)
- Write the party information on Swiss postcards.

Dress Options
- Ski fashions
- Tyrolean costumes

Decor
- Fireplace (fake or real)
- Huge, paper snowflakes
- Swiss travel posters
- Art depicting mountain scenes
- Chalet, lodge, or gasthaus atmosphere
- Candles and twinkle lights
- Ski gear and apparel
- Cuckoo clocks

Activities
- Watch ski slides or movies.
- Have a fireside sing-along.
- Hire musicians to entertain and give yodeling lessons.
- Cook and chat.

Refreshments
- Brought by guests: an assigned amount of fondue ingredients (meat, vegetables, fruit), chopped and prepared for cooking or dipping
- Provided by host: fondue equipment, cheese, bread, chocolate for dessert dips, wine, and/or hot (Swiss, of course) chocolate

Prizes/Favors
- Anything made in Switzerland: chocolate, cheese, watches, trinkets
- Fondue equipment
- Piggy banks labeled "Swiss Bank" with a few coins included (Swiss francs, if possible)

INTERNATIONAL FOOD FEST

For this festive food cooking/tasting party, each guest or couple brings the ingredients for a dish (or a completed dish) representative of their own or favorite ethnic background. During the party, guests share the traditions or tales associated with each recipe.

Invitation Ideas
- Format the invitations as recipe cards and trim them with international flags.
- Use a map to frame the invitations.
- Tuck each invitation inside a colorful travel brochure.
- Along with the invitations, enclose food items, such as pasta, bread sticks, or fortune cookies; mail in padded envelopes, pizza boxes, or small cartons.

Dress Options
- Authentic costumes of recipe origin
- As a chef wearing national colors

Decor
- Potluck decorations: guests bring corresponding ethnic decorations
- Around-the-World food stations, decorated with props
- Flags and travel posters for each country represented
- Sidewalk cafe sets
- Waitstaff dressed in international costumes

Activities
- Demonstrate food preparations as the guests cook their dishes.
- Listen to ethnic music.
- Dance ethnic dances.
- Sample all dishes and vote for "bests."
- Award prizes in a variety of categories: the spiciest, the most unusual, and so on.

Refreshments
- International food and beverages as supplied by guests

Prizes/Favors
- Cookbooks
- Recipe organizers
- Travel books
- Ethnic music on record or tape
- A booklet including the recipes for all dishes made at the party

For occasions appropriate to this theme, see the theme grid on page 188.

CASINO/GAMBLING

This is probably today's most popular theme with groups of all types and ages, gathered for any reason. Folks love to take a chance without investing real money—in other words, just for the fun of it. Most casino parties feature a shopping spree finale for guests to spend their winnings.

Invitation Ideas
- Attach a poker chip or a playing card to each invitation.
- Format the invitations to look like playing cards, and glue a picture of the guest of honor where the drawing of the "king" or "queen" would go. (If honoring a couple, make both "king" and "queen" cards.) Write the party information on the front or back of each card.
- Design the invitations to look like bingo cards; write the party information in the squares.

Dress Options
- Formal wear, á la Monte Carlo
- Casual clothing, today's casino costume in most gambling establishments

Decor
- Huge cardboard cutouts of playing cards, dice, poker chips (See Resources, #3.)
- Gaming tables
- *Wheel of Fortune* money wheel
- Lighted marquee
- Servers dressed as dealers: white tops, black bottoms, green visors, and so on

Activities
- Play various games of chance.
- Listen to music and dance.
- Play a "card" game: Give each guest a name tag made out of a miniature playing card. Have the guests team up with others to create winning poker hands; tell them to report to a moderator to be eligible for a grand-prize drawing.
- Organize an end-of-the games auction, so the guests can spend their winnings.
- Invite a local blackjack expert to teach a crash course.

Refreshments
- Finger-food appetizers and usual party fare, served at grazing stations (Don't serve a sit-down meal because guests want to stay at the playing tables. You might have servers walk around with trays of appetizers and drinks.)

Prizes/Favors
- Books, videos, and tapes on "how-to-win" at various gambling activities
- Fuzzy dice and playing cards
- Lottery tickets

For occasions appropriate to this theme, see the theme grid on page 188. **85**

CIRCUS, CIRCUS

Big kids, little kids, all kids love a circus. In fact, many have dreams of running away to join one. Your guests won't have to run far to join your circus party, nor will they have to pack a suitcase and empty their piggy banks.

Invitation Ideas
- Write the party information on deflated balloons, and send in envelopes made out of colorful, circus-themed gift wrap. (See Resources, #46.)
- Design the invitations to look like greeting cards, with black-and-white coloring-book drawings of clowns on the front cover and the party information written inside (inviting guests to the Greatest Show on _____[your street]). Attach a color crayon or two with ribbon to each invitation; wrap in tissue paper; and mail in sturdy, construction-paper envelopes.
- Record an RSVP voice-mail message with circus music in the background.

Dress Options
- As carnival barker, clown, trapeze artist, lion tamer, or other circus performer

Decor
- Circus posters and banners (See Resources, #9.)
- Ticket booth at the front door
- If outdoors: tents and canopies in primary colors
- Balloons and streamers
- Any circus equipment, costumes, or props
- Giant clown shoes for trick flower arrangements (See Resources, #6.)

Activities
- Videotape performances of all entertainers.
- Play carnival games, such as ring toss, bean bag toss, knock-over-the-bottle.
- Take instant photos of guests in front of a circus backdrop with an event banner.
- Teach or take lessons in the application of clown makeup.
- Play circus calliope-hurdy-gurdy music.
- Award prizes for best (guests') circus performances.

Refreshments
- Cotton candy, minidoughnuts, popcorn, peanuts, soda pop, and ice cream—all served circus-style in cardboard containers

Prizes/Favors
- Instant photos of guests in costumes
- Gag gifts: giant neckties, fright wigs, big clown glasses
- Tickets to the circus
- Circus toy collectibles
- Small packets of antacid tablets

For occasions appropriate to this theme, see the theme grid on page 188.

COMEDY

Funny business at its best, with lots of laughs for, by, and about the guests as they get the chance to pay tribute to comic characters, comedians, and humor. Seriously, now!

Invitation Ideas
- Mat the invitations on sheets of Sunday comics or pages from comic books (you can make the envelopes out of these as well).
- Write the party information using corny puns and one-liners, such as "Bring your significant other . . . please!"

Dress Options
- As favorite comic-strip character, comedian, or funny television personality

Decor
- The funny papers
- Banners with funny one-liners
- Silly posters and photos
- Comedy stage with microphone

Activities
- Hire a professional standup comic to entertain at the party.
- Have guests perform standup routines of their choice or host's scripts.
- Play the matching game: Write punch lines on half of the name tags, and attach cartoon pictures to the other half. Hand them all out and have the guests make matches; tell them to report to a moderator to be eligible for a grand-prize drawing.
- Play comedy trivia games.

Refreshments
- Foods with as many gag or pun names as you think your guests can "swallow"—any kind of Corn, Ham, Belly, Gut-Splitting, Knee-Slapping menu items
- Beverages served in the Punch Line

Prizes/Favors
- Tickets to comedy clubs
- T-shirts with jokes on them
- Goofy hats
- Humor albums or videos
- Joke books and calendars
- Gag gifts

For occasions appropriate to this theme, see the theme grid on page 188. **87**

CRUISE SHIP/ NAUTICAL

You might not really be sailing down the river, on the ocean, or even in the bay, but you can still throw a cruisin' party. When your guests get all decked out in *Love Boat* finery, they will have a fabulous, sea-going time.

Invitation Ideas
- Design the invitations to look and read like a cruise-ship itinerary.
- Attach a white LifeSaver candy to each invitation.
- Send the invitations in cruise-ship brochures or ticket envelopes.

Dress Options
- Nautical whites, navy blue with gold trim
- As a crew member
- As a native of a popular port

Decor
- Welcome Aboard sign over the front door
- Recording of ship's whistle
- Confetti, balloons, and streamers
- Bon Voyage signs and banners
- Travel posters
- Anchors, life preservers, netting, deck chairs
- Ports-of-call scenes arranged for photo shoots, with a backdrop of U.S.S. (guest-of-honor's name)

Activities
- Organize shuffleboard tournaments and card games.
- Dance to the music of ship's entertainers (live or recorded).
- Stage a passengers' talent show.
- Teach or take arts-and-crafts lessons.
- Have photo sessions in arranged settings.

Refreshments
- Lavish buffet with ice sculpture, fresh flowers, and beautiful foods
- Exotic drinks served in decorative containers with little umbrellas

Prizes/Favors
- Gift packs of LifeSavers candy
- Gold fish crackers
- Captains hats
- T-shirts or hats with U.S.S. ____ (guest-of-honor's name) written on them

For occasions appropriate to this theme, see the theme grid on page 188.

FAIR, COUNTY OR STATE

Every summer throngs of people enjoy the fun, food, and excitement of a state or county fair. You can stage a minifair in a backyard, parking lot, school yard, or nearby park.

Invitation Ideas
- Attach a first-prize blue ribbon or an entry blank for an official fair competition to each invitation.
- Send the invitations in minidoughnut or popcorn bags, on which you've written "Come and fill me up!"

Dress Options
- Sunday, go-to-meetin' clothes
- Farm/country garb: plaid shirts, overalls, cotton dresses, straw hats
- As a fair concessionaire

Decor
- Concession stands and game booths
- Judging tables for food and handicraft contests
- Posters and signs for fair activities
- Picnic tables with checked tablecloths
- Wild flowers, fruit, and vegetables arranged in miniature milk cans, inverted straw hats, milk buckets, old-fashioned wooden fruit and vegetable baskets

Activities
- Play all the concession games, and award trophies for game winners.
- Judge food and handicraft contests and award prizes.
- Square and line dance.
- Wait in line for specialty foods.

Refreshments
- Food stations: popcorn, cotton candy, minidoughnuts, ice cream, hot dogs, hamburgers, and beverages of host's choice
- Prize-winning contest entries: pies, cakes, cookies, jellies, pickles, breads, and fresh fruits

Prizes/Favors
- Gift-wrapped portions of prize-winning contest entries
- Blue ribbons and trophies
- Photos of guests in concession-booth settings

For occasions appropriate to this theme, see the theme grid on page 188.

FARM LIFE

Plan an authentic, down-on-the-farm get-together for hicks and slickers alike—to sit around and compare notes about the harvest, the big windstorm, or the winter ahead. Serve up thrashers'-crew helpings of home-style foods, down-home decorations, and right rural recreation.

Invitation Ideas
- For each invitation, glue a packet of vegetable seeds on a sheet of brightly colored construction paper, and add a caption like "Plant these seeds; your beans will grow. We're having a farm fest; be sure 'n' show!" or your own corny poem.
- Mat the invitations on old catalog pages, farm reports, or fabrics such as gingham, burlap, muslin, or denim.

Dress Options
- For men: jeans, overalls, and shirts
- For women: cotton dresses and aprons or frocks made from floral flour sacks
- Straw hats and kerchiefs for both

Decor
- Straw stacks and hay bales (see Party How-To's, #8), fencing, old gates
- Equipment: tractor seats, wagon wheels, hoes, rakes, kerosene lamps (empty!)
- Tables covered with quilts, embroidered cloths, crocheted runners, or doilies
- Milk cans filled with tall wheat or corn stalks
- Seed and equipment posters
- An old trough filled with ice for cold drinks
- First-prize blue ribbons

Activities
- Have square dancing and singing in the moonlight (or any kind of light).
- Organize contests: corn shucking, hog calling, rooster crowing, cow milking (real or improvised), pie eating, gunny-sack racing, horseshoe throwing, dipper-full-of-water relay racing.
- Take photos of the contest winners and interview them for the *Barnyard Bugler*

Refreshments
- Potluck menu of everything homemade, home-baked, or home-brewed (each guest brings a basket or box lunch to share with a favorite feller or gal)
- Food served in crockery dishes, enamelware, mismatched china and cut-glass bowls

Prizes/Favors
- Fresh jams and jellies
- Plants and seeds
- Dried-flower bunches
- Gift certificates to farmers' markets
- Baked goods wrapped in checkered, cloth napkins

For occasions appropriate to this theme, see the theme grid on page 188.

FORTUNE TELLING

They say, "Don't look back," so why not just look straight ahead at a party filled with fortunes and fantasies? Intrigue and mystify your guests with a glimpse into their futures. This is an excellent theme for a special get-together or a party given for an avid fan of the occult, as well as for the skeptic.

Invitation Ideas
- Write the party information on strips of paper and insert them into fortune cookies. (See Resources, #23.) Mail in small boxes to protect the cookies from breaking.
- Send the invitations in Crystal Ball envelopes. (See Party How-To's, #1.)
- Send the invitations in small boxes along with a handful of Lucky Charms cereal.

Dress Options
- As a fortune teller, Gypsy, star-gazer, or wizard
- Costumes representing a peek into the future—realistic or fantasized

Decor
- Crystal balls, Gypsy shawls, beaded curtains
- Circus fortune-teller posters
- Round, skirted tables
- Fish bowls inverted over shiny stars-and-moon decorations to represent crystal balls
- Old silk flowers tied with ribbons and lace
- Tarot cards fanned out on tables covered with tapestries, shawls, and old lace
- Candles and low-light lamps

Activities
- Have professional fortune tellers do their stuff.
- Play the Ouija Board or read each other's Chinese Fortune Cards.
- Listen and dance to Gypsy music.

Refreshments:
- Host's choice or potLUCK meal served buffet style

Prizes/Favors
- Tarot cards
- Fortune cookies with lottery numbers
- Tea cup-and-saucer sets
- Computerized horoscopes and tarot readings

KARAOKE/ STAR SEARCH

It's the rage of the country—sing-along karaoke (pronounced kah-RO-kee) parties where anyone can be a star, a back-up singer, a contest judge, a talent scout, or part of the audience. Caution: Once the guests start singing, there's no stoppin' 'em.

Invitation Ideas
- Design the invitations to look like audition announcements, and sprinkle them with tiny stars (glued or drawn on, not loose).
- Wrap each invitation around a plastic microphone (sprayed silver) and send in a padded envelope. (See Resources, #8.)
- With each invitation, enclose a song list from which guests select a song to prepare for their debut and a name tag designed as a backstage pass.
- Record the invitations on audiocassettes; record a matching RSVP voice-mail message.

Dress Options
- As an artist who usually sings the chosen song
- As a celebrity judge, talent scout, or famous audience member

Decor
- Ministage with glitter curtain, spotlights, banner, "recording" light
- Karaoke setup (can be rented in most towns) (See Resources, #33.)
- Inflatable or real musical instruments
- Concert posters, sheet music, record-album covers
- Lighted marquee on front lawn
- CD mobiles hanging from ceilings

Activities
- Stage a star-studded, fun-filled variety show complete with gong!
- Videotape all performances and "celebrity" interviews; view them during dessert.
- Play recording-star trivia games.

Refreshments
- A bountiful "sing for your supper" buffet of pile 'em yourself sandwiches, fruits and vegetables, coffee and desserts

Prizes/Favors
- Video or cassette recordings of guests' performances
- Star-shaped pillows, paper weights, picture frames, key chains, and so on
- Photos of guests in costumes, framed in CD frames
- Tapes of background music
- T-shirts or hats with star motif

KINDERGARTEN

This creative and colorful theme with a play school, arts and crafts motif is plenty of fun for kids ages one to 100. Ideally, outdoor events should be set in a picnic/play area near a playground. Indoors or outdoors, this theme is a natural for children and is equally successful for adults.

Invitation Ideas
- Make invitations out of kindergartners' artwork made with construction paper, crayons, string, and peppermint paste. You can arrange to have a local preschool class create them (offer the kids prizes, making sure that everyone gets something).
- Write the party information and address envelopes with crayons; make the writing look like kid handwriting.

Dress Options
- T-shirts, shorts, and sneakers
- Fashions decorated with popular kids' character logos or art: Barney, Disney, Sesame Street, or OshKosh by Gosh

Decor
- Lots of kids' artwork, books, toys, balloons and streamers
- Posters of children's movies and popular movie and cartoon characters
- Tables set with brightly colored party goods, plastic and paper

Activities
- Play Pin the Tail on the Donkey; Blindman's Bluff; Duck, Duck, Gray Duck; and other popular kids' games.
- Do arts and crafts.
- Have snack time.
- Tell and listen to stories during story time.
- Nap on rugs or blankies (especially after a few cocktails).
- Give awards to prize-winning "kiddies."

Refreshments
- Help-yourself finger foods, such as peanut-butter-and-jelly sandwiches, chips, Popsicles, raisins, Fruit Roll-Ups, fruit and veggies, graham and animal crackers
- Hot dogs, hamburgers, pizza, and other fast-food fare, served in kids' meal boxes
- Soda, KoolAid, or milk, along with adult beverages
- Fun desserts, sundae bar

Prizes/Favors
- Hats and T-shirts
- Big-kids toys, games, and books

For occasions appropriate to this theme, see the theme grid on page 188.   **93**

MAGIC

Create a magical, mystical party with tricks, illusions, and miracles to amuse and delight guests of all ages. Choose any theme currently associated with magic: black hats, wands, and white gloves, or the Merlin theme, with pointed hats, moons, and stars.

Invitation Ideas
- Use Magical Invitations. (See Party How-To's, #5.)
- Decorate the invitations with stars, top hats, wands, bunnies, or white gloves, using clip art, hand drawings, stickers, or rubber stamps.
- Write the party information using lemon juice, which will appear when held up to heat (be sure to give your guests instructions!).
- Send the invitations in black envelopes (make them yourself, if necessary); write the addresses using silver paint and glitter.

Dress Options
- As a sorcerer, Houdini escape artist, magician, or magician's assistant
- Bunny suit

Decor
- Stars, magic wands, pop-out flowers, rabbits in top hats
- Old theater posters of magic shows
- Magicians' props: an old trunk, a stage with a shimmery curtain backdrop
- Feather flowers in "mirrored" (Mylar-covered) containers

Activities
- Have the guests perform amazing and amusing feats (which they prepare ahead of time).
- Hire a professional magician to really dazzle and bewilder your guests.
- Play the matching game: Have the guests match "magical" words (such as "disappear," "illusion," "trick," "escape") to song, book, movie, or product titles.

Refreshments
- A favorite menu arrayed on a table covered with a black tablecloth and standing against a black backdrop (so the food looks as though it is floating)
- Special snacks served on Mylar paper, laid on a clean and shiny magician's saw
- Snacks served in inverted top hats lined with aluminum foil
- Napkins held together by small, metal, magic tricks

Note: Plant a few "disappearing liquid" glasses among the regular glasses.

Prizes/Favors
- Magic markers and Magic Slates
- Rabbit's-foot charms
- Magic tricks

For occasions appropriate to this theme, see the theme grid on page 188.

MYSTERY

Throw a party for whodunit buffs who show up with their wits sharpened to solve a mystery, even if they "haven't a clue." This theme is a tribute to all famous detectives, cops, or mystery masters from books, movies, television, or the nostalgic radio era.

Invitation Ideas
- Write the party information as a series of clues, clearly directing guests to the party; use such mystery terms as "clues," "suspect," "sleuth, "solve," and "crime."
- Attach a tiny magnifying glass to each invitation.
- Decorate the invitations and envelopes with fingerprints.

Note: See the Magic party (page 94) for additional invitation and envelope ideas.

Dress Options
- As a famous character from the world of mystery

Decor
- Posters and photos of mystery books, shows, movies, authors, and characters
- Props and wardrobe items, such as guns (fake!), trench coats, hats, newspapers with peephole cutouts, old shoes with gum on the soles, magnifying-glass-shaped picture frames holding collages of the guest of honor
- Name tags decorated with tiny magnifying glasses
- Body outline drawn on living room floor, crime area taped off with yellow tape
- Box covers of the game Clue used as the focal point of the table centerpiece
- Enlarged replicas of Clue playing tokens: rope, knife, gun, poison bottle
- Candelabra with cobwebs on it
- Each table centerpiece dedicated to a different detective

Activities
- Play the matching game: Write clues on half the name tags, and solutions on the other half. Have the guests find their match. For example: A clue, such as "substance that keeps balloons afloat" matches the solution "helium."
- Play a game that duplicates the eight characters of a Home Mystery game, for a lively progressive dinner game. (See Party Tips, #7.)
- Award grand prizes to guests who solve the mysteries.

Refreshments
- Food with such names as Columbo's Combo, Ellery's Celery, Matlock's Meat Loaf, Mrs. Fletcher's Fruit Cup, The Commish's Knishes, Perry's Perrier, Pink Panther Punch, Mike Hammer's Rusty Nails, Charlie Chan's Champagne

Prizes/Favors
- Kojak's lollipops
- Video- or audiotapes of mystery programs
- Paperback mysteries
- Clue games

For occasions appropriate to this theme, see the theme grid on page 188. **95**

OVER-THE-HILL

Don't ask why, but people turning thirty consider themselves going "over-the-hill." I don't think so! But, for some humorous poking-of-fun at aging, pull out all the gag gifts and paint the town black to help your guest of honor mourn the end of a decade and salute the beginning of another.

Invitation Ideas
- Wrap each invitation in a black arm band, for mourning.
- Send the invitations in black envelopes or in envelopes made from magazine ads for "mature" products.

Dress Options
- All-black clothing
- As an old codger, walker and all

Decor
- Black crepe paper draped all over the place
- A shrine of the guest-of-honor's photo, with black cloth draped around it
- Displays of old-folks gear: Geritol, denture cleaner, hearing aids, prune juice, hair dye, eye glasses, and support hose
- Posters and advertising art from retirement homes, senior citizen publications, social security information
- R.I.P. markers and a rocking chair bearing the guest-of-honor's name
- Ace bandages wrapped around legs of the serving table, to help it stand
- Fake false teeth as napkin holders

Activities
- Open gag gifts.
- Play the name-tag game: Make a list of names and titles of songs, books, movies, and television shows that contain the word "old." Write half of each name or title of one name tag and the other half on another name tag. Distribute the tags to your guests and have them find matches. (See Party Tips, #4, 7.)
- Slooooooooow dance.
- Midway through the party, give prizes to guests who still remember and can quickly recite their mate/date's name, birth date, anniversary, and social security number. (See Resources, #40, 58, for more ideas.)

Refreshments
- Old Dutch Potato Chips, Old Milwaukee Beer, and so on
- Strained foods (Provide a personalized bib for the guest of honor.)

Prizes/Favors
- Black arm bands and false teeth
- Instant photos of guests with the guest of honor

For occasions appropriate to this theme, see the theme grid on page 188.

PAJAMA

A theme for morning, noon, or overnight. Guests of all ages slip into their "jammies," nighties (or even naughties for the daring), and big, funny slippers for a sleepy-time party, complete with pillow fights and bedtime stories.

Invitation Ideas
- Tuck the invitations into small flannel nightcaps.
- Cut out pieces of flannel in the shape of nightcaps and glue them to the front of each invitation.
- Take a photo of guest(s) of honor in pajamas; photocopy and use as invitation covers.

Dress Options
- Pajamas, nightgowns, fuzzy slippers, or creative variations

Decor
- Pillows, "blankies," sleeping bags
- Sleepwear or bedding posters and sleep-related advertisements on walls
- Mattresses, sofas, chaise lounges, and daybeds made up for sleeping
- Wall hangings: magazine photos of "sleeping beauties" (people, animals, cartoons) matted on pillowcases
- Sheets and bedspreads covering tables, pillowcases for chair covers
- Flowers arranged in bedroom slippers

Activities
- Greet guests with lullaby music.
- Sing "sleep" or "good night" songs.
- Play board games and charades.
- Have pillow fights.
- Parade pajama fashions.
- Read or tell bedtime or scary stories.
- Award prizes for all activities.

Refreshments
- Bedtime snacks and the spoils of a midnight refrigerator raid
- Breakfast fare: pancakes, waffles, French toast
- Warm milk, hot cocoa
- Menu of host's choice served on breakfast trays

Prizes/Favors
- Novelty pajamas
- Bedtime storybooks
- Relaxation tapes
- Snoring preventatives

For occasions appropriate to this theme, see the theme grid on page 188.

STARRY SUMMER'S NIGHT

A heaven-sent, romantic, star-sprinkled, and, possibly, star-studded, theme for dinner parties, galas, or any trip-to-the-stars gathering taking place in a backyard, on a deck or patio, or at the poolside. Couples celebrating an engagement, wedding, or anniversary will be honored to be honored with this party theme.

Invitation Ideas
- Make formal white invitations, professionally printed or handwritten, trimmed with glitter, star confetti, and Mylar ribbon.
- Fold the invitations into star shapes and trim as above.
- Send the invitations in elegantly addressed envelopes decorated with rubber stamps and glitter. (Do not put confetti or stars in envelopes because this has proven to be annoying, rather than festive, for the recipient.)

Dress Options
- Semiformal or formal, as desired
- Any clothing with a star motif

Decor
- If inside or under a tent, glow-in-the-dark stars and constellations attached to the ceiling, or projected onto the ceiling using gobo light, and white or star-flecked tulle generously draped and wrapped around tent or lightposts
- Table set with the best linens, crystal, china, and flatware, with Mylar, star-shaped place cards
- Mirrored votive candles
- Floral arrangements trimmed with star garlands
- Twinkle lights and luminaria bags with star cutouts (See Party How-To's, #9.)

Activities
- Listen and dance to live or recorded music: harp, violin, piano, or orchestra.
- Star gaze though a telescope.
- Hire a What's in the Stars? fortune teller (or have a guest play the part).
- Videotape interviews á la *Lifestyles of the Rich and Famous*.
- Play Name That Tune: Play tunes that have the word "star" in the title.

Refreshments
- Lovely dinner, served sit-down or buffet style

Prizes/Favors
- Anything star-shaped: paper weights, notepads, faux jewels
- Instant photos of guests, presented in star-shaped frames
- Individual horoscope printouts
- Grand prize: A star in the National Registry (See Resources, #19.)

For occasions appropriate to this theme, see the theme grid on page 188.

SURFIN' USA

The surf's up, so get ready for the big one! Party, that is. This is one of the most-frequently produced party themes in the world. Ever since Gidget fell in love with Moon Doggie, the life of a beach bum has beckoned those who long to loaf around until the next ocean wave comes rolling in.

Invitation Ideas
- Send the invitations in see-through envelopes filled with bits of sand, shells, coral critters, and plant life. (See Resources, #29.)
- Write the party information on postcards from the West Coast.
- Record an RSVP voice-mail message with Beach Boys background music.

Dress Options
- Surfin' duds: bathing suits, bikinis, wet suits
- Tank shirts, cut-off jeans, sandals

Decor
- Surf boards of every size and description
- Sand piles, sea shells, starfish
- Fish netting draped on walls, over tables, in doorways
- Travel posters featuring beaches
- Mobiles of 45 records
- LP photo-album covers
- Beach towels, huge sunglasses, bright straw hats
- Beach chairs and umbrellas
- A beach booth for trinkets, lotions, drinks

Activities
- Dance to Beach Boys' songs and other sixties hits.
- Play volleyball and tug of war.
- Have beach-ball-balance relay contests.
- Build sand castles.

Refreshments
- Snacks served in sand pails or on trays made out of vintage album covers (cut out hole for cup), with terry-cloth napkins
- "Sand"wiches piled on clean surfboards
- Drinks in fun glasses, with crazy straws or umbrellas

Prizes/Favors
- Super-cool sunglasses
- Vintage movie posters
- Videos of "beach" movies
- Beach Boys tapes or CDs
- Instant photos of guests

For occasions appropriate to this theme, see the theme grid on page 188.

TACKY/TASTELESS

Get decked out in your worst! High-water polyesters; plaid, three-piece pantsuits; frumpy frocks; and fizzled fashions come out of mothballs or the thrift store. The gents slick down their hair, adjust their horn-rimmed glasses, and position their pocket protectors, while the femmes fatales (or is it "fatal") fluff up their frizzy do's and trim the snags from their polyester finery to party "out of style."

Invitation Ideas
- Tuck the invitations into plastic pocket protectors; label each with a guest's name.
- Print the party information on old letterhead; send in nonmatching envelopes.
- Attach a neon hair bow or an obnoxiously loud tie to each invitation and send in a used padded envelope, with former address label blacked out.

Dress Options
- Any color, print, or combination of patterns and colors that will offend the eye
- Ill-fitting and out-of-style garments and shoes

Decor
- Tablecloths made out of fabrics with clashing colors and garish prints
- Clunky, cheap vases filled with dreadful plastic flowers
- White elephant eyesores from the attic and closet
- Items with product or place logos—especially condiments, napkins, place mats, towels, or serving ware
- Leftover Christmas or other holiday decorations

Activities
- Display uncouth behavior. For example: Order a pizza and eat it in front of others without offering to share. Be sure not to use a napkin!
- Award prizes (such as trophies with wrong or misspelled names) for the Nerdiest or Tackiest costumes or behaviors.
- Exchange tacky, tasteless gifts.
- As a final tacky gesture, appear in pajamas as a go-home hint to the guests.

Note: This party makes a delightful fund-raiser: Guests convince others to take the tacky items they have brought, offering money. All the money goes to charity.

Refreshments
- Tacky foods in mismatched dishes, buckets, baskets, or boxes
- Regional likeness of "gut bombs" or "sliders" (White Castle hamburgers), grandiosely presented on brand-new garbage can lids
- Beverages served in fruit jars, plastic cups, or glasses with advertising logos

Prizes/Favors
- All your tasteless decorations
- Doggy bags filled with leftovers
- Gifts wrapped in (wrong) holiday paper, newspaper, or brown bags

For occasions appropriate to this theme, see the theme grid on page 188.

THIS IS YOUR LIFE

Patterned after the TV classic show, this is an ideal theme concept for a milestone birthday, retirement, or anniversary celebration. Producing the surprise tribute takes extensive planning and choreographing, but it will be more than well-worth the effort.

Invitation Ideas
* Enclose a blank photo page with each invitation, instructing the guests to complete the page with photo, poem, writing, or drawing for a This Is Your Life keepsake album to be presented to the guest of honor. (Guests can mail their page back or bring it along to the party.)

Dress Options
* Host's choice
* Costume from the era when guest first met the guest of honor

Decor
* TV set and a This Is Your Life backdrop
* Curtain or screen concealing surprise guests
* Stage with chairs for the guest of honor and surprise guests
* Audience seating
* Photo blowups that record the life progression of the guest of honor

Activities
* Surprise the guest of honor with a This Is Your Life presentation.
* Play audio- and videotaped messages from people who could not attend, immediately after introducing the person with a clue, such as "...and now we have a message from someone who was a favorite roller-skating partner."
* Party, reminisce, and socialize.

Refreshments
* Host's choice, guest-of-honor's favorite menu

Prizes/Favors
* Instant photos of guests with the guest of honor
* Life's record-keeping booklets (obtained from insurance company)
* Address/telephone books

For occasions appropriate to this theme, see the theme grid on page 188.

PREHISTORIC/ FLINTSTONES

Yabadaba Doo! This party theme can be patterned after the era, the cartoon, or the movie. Just making a list of "rock" and "stone" gimmick sayings will keep you busy for awhile—"Eat at the Soft Rock Cafe," "Come to a rock-a-bye baby shower," "Wear stone-washed jeans," and hundreds more! Tune in to the next *Flintstones* TV episode, and you'll get dozens of ideas.

Invitation Ideas
- Write the party information on faux rocks, and send them in cardboard cartons. (See Resources, #28.)
- Attach a small toy dinosaur to each invitation, or decorate the invitations with dinosaur stickers or rubber stamps.
- Cut beige card stock into "bone" shapes; write the party information on them.
- Write the party information on foamcore (a flat, smooth Styrofoam material) that has been sprayed with granite spray. (See Resources, #28.)

Dress Options
- Rockin' Stone Age rags and skins
- As a character from the *Flintstones*

Decor
- Rocks, stones, skins, bones, inflatable dinosaurs
- Prehistoric/Stone Age posters, *Flintstones* movie posters
- *Flintstones* comic-book-page blowups
- Signs: Bone Appetite, Bedrock Room, Livingstone Room, and so on

Activities
- Listen and dance to rock and roll music.
- Pitch pebbles and juggle fake rocks.
- Watch movies (dinosaur, Stone Age, and *Flintstones*), or just have them playing in the background.
- Photograph guests in costumes.

Refreshments
- Foods with such names as Dino Dogs, Barney Burgers, Potato Pebbles, Granite Gravy, Boney Baloney, Stone-Ground Bread, Rock Candy, Rocky Road Ice Cream
- Drinks on the rocks

Prizes/Favors
- Polished-rock magnets, paper weights, and jewelry
- Dinosaur novelty items
- Pumice stone, rock-crystal bath salts

For occasions appropriate to this theme, see the theme grid on page 188.

TOGA

This theme is popular among the campus crowd, especially fraternity and sorority members. A guest need only wear a sheet to fulfill the costume requirement. Baby boomer college alumni will love this theme party because it conjures up vivid memories of their days (and nights) at school.

Invitation Ideas
- Print the party information on parchment paper, roll into scrolls, tie with gold ribbons, and send in cardboard tubes.
- Make formal invitations, and trim them with gold laurel leaves.
- Write the party information to look like Greek lettering.

Dress Options
- White sheet, secured with a gold cord, and sandals

Decor
- Greek columns (plastic, cardboard, paper.)
- Posters of the Greek gods
- Greek travel posters (especially of the various Greek ruins)
- Artwork depicting ancient Greece
- Sundials, telescopes
- White sheets draped over doorways and tables

Activities
- Have gladiator games, competing for gold coins (remove all breakables!).
- Give and take footbaths and massages.
- Organize grape peeling contests.
- Play dice games.
- Go for a Passeggiata (stroll) before dinner (the neighbors will love this).
- Dance, dance, dance.
- Play Name the Gods: Match the names of the gods to their titles. For example: Zeus, the ruler of the gods; Hades, the ruler of the underworld; Aphrodite, the goddess of love; and so on.

Refreshments
- Popular party food, such as popcorn, pretzels, chips, hamburgers, hot dogs, or pizza, with a sampling of Greek fare (See Greek party, page 80.)
- French fries, since they were invented in Greece

Note: For the really nostalgic frat party touch, beer, and more beer

Prizes/Favors
- Gold bracelets
- Batches of baklava
- Gold-coin jewelry or desk accessories
- Booklet of Greek recipes
- Miniature sundials

For occasions appropriate to this theme, see the theme grid on page 188.

MEDIEVAL

Your guests will join King Arthur at his Round Table, as did the knights, knaves, ladies, and wenches of medieval days. In spite of the men's steel armor and women's tight-cinched bodices, they managed to have a raucous time.

Invitation Ideas
- Write the party information on parchment paper, roll them up scroll-style, and fasten with a blob of wax and your seal. Send in cardboard tubes.
- Keep the invitations flat, and make matching parchment envelopes sealed as above. (See Resources, #46.)
- Hand-address each invitation in a medieval-looking script.

Dress Options
- As royalty, in rich garments and jewels
- As peasants or serfs, in modest rags

Decor
- Real or painted tapestries, stained glass, and banners
- Candles on candelabras
- Warriors' shields, real or painted (dragon, griffin, and/or unicorn insignia)
- Wooden picnic-style tables and benches (or one big, round table, if possible)
- Tankards and goblets filled with fresh flowers
- Boar's head for centerpiece

Activities
- Listen and dance to music of the period, live or recorded.
- Watch jesters and mimes, troubadours or minstrels (hire professionals or appoint guests for these roles).
- Stage jousts.
- Play checkers, chess, and backgammon.
- Eat and drink to excess, with little regard to table etiquette!

Refreshments
- Turkey drumsticks, pot pies, coarse breads, fruit, and cheese
- Cider, ale, and wine in pewter mugs

Note: Serve knives and spoons only. (Forks weren't invented yet!)

Prizes/Favors
- Hand-tooled leather items
- Instant photos of guests in costumes
- Pewter frames or mugs
- Wishes for the guest of honor, written on parchment and signed by all the guests
- Bottles or packets of exotic spices

For occasions appropriate to this theme, see the theme grid on page 188.

VICTORIAN

Harken back to the era of Queen Victoria, with all its propriety and formality. This theme works very well for a wedding, afternoon tea, or costume ball for guests who love to dress up and drift back in time. If at all possible, hold this party in a mansion or a Victorian home.

Invitation Ideas
- Make formal, handwritten invitations out of off-white or ecru-colored paper; trim with lace, ribbons, and small flowers.
- For a tea party, enclose a decoratively packaged tea bag with each invitation.

Dress Options
- Authentic vintage costumes
- Hats for ladies and gents
- All-beige and/or -white clothing
- Parasols and fans

Decor
- Antique furniture and paintings arranged for photo settings
- Vintage clothing, shoes, hats, and jewelry either hanging on walls or arranged in decorative groupings
- Tables covered with damask linens and/or crocheted and lace tablecloths
- Doilies, handkerchiefs, and lace runners under serving dishes
- Flowers—dried and artificial—mixed with fresh, arranged in antique silver pieces, crockery, baskets, crystal, or china
- Floral fabric or fresh greens and blossoms swagged over doorways and windows
- Ornately framed photos or antique postcards displayed decoratively

Activities
- Photocopy pages from old catalogs (found in libraries) of items that no longer exist (especially medical devices), covering the names of the items. Have guests identify them and their functions.
- Sing Victorian-era songs (provide song sheets). For example: "God Save the Queen," "The Band Played On," "By the Light of the Silvery Moon."
- For ladies' groups: Give fan-flirting lessons. (See Party How-To's, #14.)
- Go on horse-and-carriage rides, if possible.

Refreshments
- A light tea menu, luncheon, or a full, eight-course dinner served on a table fit for a queen, preferably Victoria

Prizes/Favors
- Fancy fans, with "flirting" rules
- Lace and linen handkerchiefs
- Floral and lace-trimmed sachets of potpourri
- Booklets of Victorian recipes and serving ideas

For occasions appropriate to this theme, see the theme grid on page 188.

ROARING TWENTIES

Flappers and dappers kick up their heels in a lively Charleston or Black Bottom, while hoping that the Feds won't show up to stop the party and prohibit all frivolity, fun, and frolic.

Invitation Ideas
- An offer they won't refuse: In the invitations, instruct guests to search the personals section of the local newspaper for the voice-mail number to call for further details, including the must-have password. (Be sure to place the number in the personals!)
- Enclose faux pearls and red-satin ribbon bow ties as "costume starter" suggestions. Send in padded envelopes.

Dress Options
- Ladies in roaring twenties' finery—fringy and flirty
- Gents in tuxedos or pin-striped suits

Decor
- Speakeasy peephole at the front door
- Intimate nightclub atmosphere, with white tablecloths and candles
- Small dance floor and tiny stage with a bandstand (hire a jazz band, if possible)
- Gun-check at the door
- Bathtub filled with gin, and bottles filled with ginger ale
- Fish bowls with live goldfish as table centerpieces
- Strands of pearls and red bows for napkin rings

Activities
- Have Charleston contests.
- Dance and listen to jazz (live or recorded).
- Award prizes for best costumes.
- Stage a midnight raid by Elliot Ness and his prohibition agents.
- Organize a sing-along of twenties' hits. (See Resources, #26.)

Refreshments
- Hard or soft drinks served in coffee cups
- A late-night buffet of host's choice

Prizes/Favors
- Instant photos of guests in costumes
- Art deco picture frames
- Faux pearls and red satin clip-on bow ties

FORTIES

Throw a big band bash for those who can actually remember the forties, or those who are too young to remember, but are intrigued by the era. The combination of a variety of costumes and the sound of nostalgic music will make a fantastic party.

Invitation Ideas
- Make a black-and-white photo collage of guest(s)-of-honor; reproduce to make 5-by-7-inch postcards. Write the party information on the back, using small print typically found on the blank side of a postcard.
- Enclose a dog tag, personalized with guest's name, with each invitation.

Dress Options
- Wartime uniforms
- Forties fashions—dressy or casual
- As a movie star of the era

Decor
- Props to recreate a stage door canteen, Red Cross center, or military set
- Ballroom with a bandstand and revolving mirror ball
- Forties movie posters, photos, and memorabilia
- Wartime signs and banners, Uncle Sam posters, flags
- Red, white, and blue balloons, crepe paper streamers

Activities
- Dance till dawn to live or recorded music.
- Play forties trivia games.
- Provide entertainment á la the Andrews Sisters.
- Sing forties songs (provide song sheets). For example: "Don't Sit Under the Apple Tree," "Mairzy Doats," "Over the Rainbow." (See Resources, #26.)

Refreshments
- Canteen fare: sandwiches, coffee and drinks, doughnuts, fruit, and ice cream
- Or a menu of host's choice served canteen (cafeteria) style
- SOS (creamed mystery meat on toast points)

Note: For an extra-authentic touch, hand out ration coupons for meals.

Prizes/Favors
- Personalized dog tags
- Videos of forties movies
- Audiocassettes of forties music
- Instant photos of guests in costumes

For occasions appropriate to this theme, see the theme grid on page 188.

FIFTIES

Sock hop around the clock to celebrate a birthday, anniversary, reunion, or even a delightful kids' party. This party theme is very popular, so the ideas for producing it are amazingly extensive.

Invitation Ideas
- Tuck each invitation into a white sock. Guests must present the sock at the door to receive its mate and another pair for a date/mate.
- Record an RSVP voice-mail message to the background music of a fifties hit.

Dress Options
- Blue jeans, T-shirts, poodle skirts, and ponytails—straight from the movie *Grease* (See Resources, #70.)

Decor
- Cardboard or paper cutouts of jukeboxes, giant phonograph records, soda fountain items, dancing couples, '57 Chevies, roller skates
- Signs with fifties sayings: Elvis is King, Rock around the Clock, At the Hop
- Posters of fifties movies and movie stars (See Resources, #10.)
- Front covers or pages of fifties magazines and newspapers
- Life-sized cutouts of James Dean, Elvis Presley, and Marilyn Monroe (See Resources, #1.)
- Balloons, streamers, and other decorations in black and white
- Black-and-white checked table covers
- Ponytail holders for napkins

Activities
- Hop and bop till you drop to recorded music or a fifties band.
- Play fifties trivia games.
- Have hula hoop contests, dance contests, and a spotlight dance (one couple dances a solo in the center of the dance floor).
- Sing fifties songs (provide song sheets). For example: "Splish Splash," "Blueberry Hill," "Party Doll," "Sixteen Tons." (See Resources, #26.)

Refreshments
- Soda fountain fare: hamburgers, sloppy joes, hot dogs, ice-cream soda, root beer floats, Cokes, and Pepsis
- Food served in plastic or paper baskets
- If regionally possible, White Castle hamburgers (sliders)
- Brownies á la mode, chocolate chip cookies

Prizes/Favors
- Instant photos with celebrity cutouts
- Fifties memorabilia
- Hop socks

For occasions appropriate to this theme, see the theme grid on page 188.

SIXTIES

Although the anniversary of Woodstock Weekend and National Hippie Day is offi-cially August 17–19, you can celebrate this occasion any time of the year. Just send out the word, and the loyal, laid-back, love-in generation will turn out for the party.

Invitation Ideas
- Decorate the invitations with photos from 1960-69 (scour your local thrift shop for old magazines).
- Make envelopes from pieces of tie-dyed sheets or paper.

Dress Options
- Bell bottoms, grungy T-shirts, crochet vests, headbands, sandals

Decor
- Beads hanging in doorways, peace signs, lava lamps (See Resources, #78.)
- Macramé wall hangings, arts-and-crafts treasures
- Sixties movie and music posters (See Resources, #10.)
- Tables covered with shawls and crochet work
- Mobile made of eight-tracks and album covers

Activities
- Have a hootenanny sing-along to a folk guitar accompaniment (provide song sheets)—anything by the Beatles, the Beach Boys, or Peter, Paul, and Mary.
- Play sixties trivia games.
- Take instant photos of guests.

Refreshments
- Healthy, natural foods, such as rice, salads, pasta, vegetables, and fruit
- Jugs filled with fresh juice—fruit and vegetable
- At least one soy recipe

Prizes/Favors
- Tapes of sixties favorites (you might have to find the eight-tracks)
- Poems or writings from the sixties
- Tie-dyed ties or scarves—they're back!

SEVENTIES

Create a little discomania with a party that pays tribute to the era of extrovert dances, outrageously "cool" fashions, and debuts of Archie Bunker, *Rocky I*, and streaking. What a sM.A.S.H.ing party this is going to be!

Invitation Ideas
- Format the invitations as menus (see Refreshments), with the food on the front cover and the party information inside.
- Make envelopes from loud-print fabric or paper.

Dress Options
- Loud, polyester, landscape prints
- Full-flared pants, open-to-the-waist shirts (for the men!)
- White *Saturday Night Fever* three-piece suits and Pee Wee Herman power pumps
- Minidresses in wild prints, platform shoes, thigh-high boots
- Clingy, flimsy, polyester evening gowns with see-through midriffs

Decor
- Posters of seventies movies, concerts, or record albums
- Record album covers as mobiles or on tables as decorative trays
- Wild-print fabrics as table and chair covers (garish, splashy sheets and pillow-cases are ideal)
- Seventies newspapers or magazines (you can use the current events, political and sports personalities, and product advertisements for a trivia game)

Activities
- Disco till dawn.
- Have a Name That Seventies Tune contest.
- Organize a Feverish Dance contest.
- Stage a fashion show, with judges.
- Compete in a Travolta Strut contest.
- View old *Saturday Night Live* and *M.A.S.H.* episodes.
- Put on a talent show, with a gong.

Refreshments
- Foods and beverages named after the movie/TV hits of the seventies: Last Mango in Paris, A Clockwork Orange, True Grits in Grease, Archie Bunker Burgers, Bolushi's Sushi, The Sting-ers, Cabaret Sauvignon, Roots Beer, The Beer Hunter, Rocky Road Ice Cream, Godfather's Goodies, Jawsbreakers

Prizes/Favors
- Videos of seventies movies or television shows
- Eight-track tapes sprayed gold

For occasions appropriate to this theme, see the theme grid on page 188.

WARTIME/M.A.S.H.

Join the staff of the Medical Auxiliary Station Hospital for fun and (war) games. Ideas for this theme are as bountiful as the laughs still being inspired by the zillion-award-winning series.

Invitation Ideas
- Mat the invitations on army-green paper or cloth, roll up, and tie each one with a dog tag. Mail in padded envelopes.

Dress Options
- War uniform
- Hospital garb (as a patient)
- As one of the key characters (Bet you a girdle you can't guess who shows up most often!)

Decor
- Barracks atmosphere: cots, pup tents, camouflage materials, military gear
- Wooden road signs
- Hospital equipment
- Balloons in camouflage design (See Resources, #9.)
- Small lamps and hanging flashlights
- Mess-hall seating
- Equipment room, for some secret smooching
- Centerpiece arrangements in boots and/or inverted helmets
- Shower/latrine set

Activities
- Dance to music of the era.
- Play *M.A.S.H.* trivia game.
- Watch favorite taped episodes.
- Have Klinger Dress-Up Relay Races: create teams and speed-dress from a bag of large-sized women's clothing and shoes, one member from each team at a time. The team whose members all finish dressing first wins a prize.

Refreshments
- Mess-hall-style service, menu of choice
- Canteens filled with both non- and alcoholic beverages
- Martinis from the still or I.V. dripper
- K rations
- Chocolate bars

Prizes/Favors
- *M.A.S.H.* hats and T-shirts
- Videotapes of favorite episodes
- *M.A.S.H.* memorabilia
- Instant photos in *M.A.S.H.* setting

For occasions appropriate to this theme, see the theme grid on page 188.

FUTURISTIC FANTASIES

Zoom into a future of space-aged technology and whimsical futuristic inventions. Have your guests come wearing costumes and carrying props or signs that predict the lifestyle of the twenty-first century, which, at the time this book is written, is less than 2,000 days away.

Invitation Ideas
- Design the invitations using state-of-the-art computer graphics, laser art, and holograms.
- Write the party information on Mylar paper, then send in clear space tubes.
- Send an "into the future" kit with each invitation: Martian "boinger" headgear (antenna-like headgear), hologram glasses, and security I.D. badge; mail everything in a pizza box (this is the best way to mail bulky invitations).
- Record an RSVP voice-mail message with *Space Odyssey* music in the background. Do some voice distortion to your message. (See Party Tips, #2.)

Dress Options
- Shiny, shimmering, reflective clothing
- *Star Trek* costumes (human and "alien")
- Representing futuristic occupations or technological developments

Decor
- Mylar and futuristic mirrored fabrics, for the party room and the serving table
- Laser lights, holograms
- Futuristic posters and art
- Drawings of futuristic inventions or technological advancements

Activities
- Write overly technical descriptions of everyday items on a sheet of paper, and include a few made-up descriptions. Have the guests guess the items.
- Hang magazine photos or drawings of ultramodern products on the wall; create teams; have the teams compete to identify the products and their uses.
- Have a *Star Trek* trivia contest.

Refreshments
- Space shuttle menu items: fruit bars, dried foods on small trays, Tang
- Foods and beverages with such names as Mars Bars, Milky Way, Lil' Orbit Doughnuts, Satellite Stew, Constellation Rations, Big Dipper Ice Cream, and Solar Cola

Prizes/Favors
- Inexpensive, state-of-the-art gimmicks or gadgets
- Mylar or hologram novelty items
- Gift certificates for space-shuttle rides

For occasions appropriate to this theme, see the theme grid on page 188.

ARTS AND CRAFTS

The whole family gets into the fun and challenge of an arts-and-crafts session. Give your guests several crafts from which to choose, and they will surely find an activity to bring out their hidden talents.

Invitation Ideas
- Decorate paper invitations with yarn, feathers, rubber stamp art, buttons, beads, and drawings.
- Make envelopes to fit your one-of-a-kind invitations. (See Resources, #46.)
- Include materials for small craft projects with your invitations; award a prize for the best completed project.

Dress Options
- Casual, easily washable clothing
- Pastel-colored shirts that other guests can decorate with washable paints
- Home-crafted or decorated clothing items to be entered into the Best Decorated Item contest

Decor
- Well-lit work tables
- A variety of craft supplies and equipment (See Resources, #76.)

Activities
- Learn or teach crafts—hire instructors, ask for volunteer help, or read craft books and teach your guests yourself.
- Guess the identity of what others have produced.
- Award prizes for craft achievement.
- Take instant photos, or videotape works in progress. (You can then watch the videos as a party activity.)

Refreshments
- Finger foods for sipping and chewing while crafting and chatting
- Cookies, cupcakes, and candies hand-decorated by the guests

Prizes/Favors
- Blue ribbons for excellence
- Crafting kits
- Discount coupons for craft supplies
- Crafting books or magazines

BOARD/PICTIONARY/ TRIVIA GAMES

Everyone will be game for this theme party: friends, family, neighbors, or work-mates. Whether you focus on just one game, such as Pictionary, or plan a total game gamut, everyone will come out a winner.

Invitation Ideas
- Attach game pieces, checkers, or dominos to the invitations.
- Format the invitations to look like a game board.
- Enclose a few pieces of play money with each invitation.

Dress Options
- Casual and comfortable clothing to accommodate possible floor or stairway seating
- Clothing that represents a game of choice

Decor
- Game boards and empty game boxes
- Game posters
- Giant game pieces
- Blowups of score sheets
- Card tables, game tables, or long bingo tables

Activities
- Assign teams—couples, men against women, kids against adults, or tournament style (whatever suits the group)—and play games!
- Award prizes.

Refreshments
- Easy-and-"neat-to-eat-while-trying-to-defeat" finger foods with such names as Trivial Pursoup, Parcheesi Crackers, Scrabble Scrapple, Checkers Chex Snacks, Dominos Pizza
- Beverages like Gatorade for the mental athletics

Prizes/Favors
- Trophies, plaques, award certificates
- Medals and ribbons á la Olympics
- Games, games, games

For occasions appropriate to this theme, see the theme grid on page 188.

BOOKS

A literary theme holds volumes of promise. You can choose a specific literary genre for your party, such as Literary Lovers, The Bards' Bash, or even Bookworm Barbecue (for the backyard bookish).

Invitation Ideas
- Make the invitations look like bookmarks, and trim with ribbon.
- Make greeting-card-style invitations, with the title of the party on the front and the party information formatted as the table of contents inside.
- Format the invitations to look like library cards.

Dress Options
- According to book theme

Decor
- Book shelves, either real or drawn to create a backdrop for the buffet or banquet table
- Books, books, books, stacked or held between bookends
- Posters from bookstores or libraries

Activities
- Play serious trivia games corresponding to the theme.
- Play the name game: Match famous authors with their books.
- Sing songs with the words "book" or "read" in the titles (give out song sheets).
- Play a book trivia game: Write book titles on strips of paper and distribute them throughout the party room. Hand out game sheets, with clues relating to the book titles, and have the guests match the clues to the books. The first guest who correctly completes the game sheet wins a prize.

Refreshments
- Host's choice, set out on a buffet table with corresponding recipe books

Prizes/Favors
- Bookmarks
- Books, corresponding to the books in the trivia game
- Books on tape
- Gift certificates to a local bookstore
- Book bags
- *Ex libris* stickers

CARD GAMES

You don't have to wait for a special occasion to get a group of friends together for an evening of lively card playing. If your favorite card shark has a special occasion in his or her cards, make the card deck the party theme and the details will fall into place, like a perfect hand.

Invitation Ideas
- Write the party information on a piece of paper the size of a playing card, make copies, and glue to the pattern sides of actual cards.
- Write the party information on the back of a score sheet, with "Let's Put Our Cards on the Table" as a header.
- Make envelopes out of the newspaper bridge section or out of wrapping paper with a playing-card design.
- Record an RSVP voice-mail message saying, "Deal me in —or out."

Dress Options
- Comfortable, casual clothing for a lot of sitting

Decor
- Huge playing cards (color blowups) on the walls
- Poker chips
- Cribbage boards
- Bridge pads
- Card tables

Activities
- Play the name-tag game: Attach a tiny playing card to each guest's name tag. Have players match up with each other to make winning poker hands. (See Party Tips, #7.)
- Play cards, cards, and more cards.
- Invite or hire an instructor or expert to give quick lessons.

Refreshments
- Finger foods, such as little sandwiches cut into heart, diamond, club, and spade shapes with cookie cutters
- Variety of beverages with long straws, for easy access
- Buffet of host's choice

Prizes/Favors
- Decks of cards
- Score pads
- Card grippers (See Resources, #3.)
- Playing card trinkets: key chains, flashlights, refrigerator magnets

    For occasions appropriate to this theme, see the theme grid on page 188.

COLLECTING

If your guest of honor is building a collection of any kind, that passion will be great subject matter for your theme party. With a little imagination even the most obscure obsession can become a remarkable motif. Collectors of stamps, coins, Barbie dolls, antiques, artwork, sports cards, or classic autos will be so excited when you surround them with their "stuff," they'll have to collect themselves.

Invitation Ideas
- Decorate invitations with collection-appropriate graphics or small, light items.
- Write the party information using such plays on words as "We're taking up a collection," "Collect your thoughts," "Don't call us collect," and so on.

Dress Options
- Anything that follows the theme: As a mail person for a stamp collector, in sports gear for a card collector, as a doll for a doll collector, and so on

Decor
- Anything related to the collectable items: catalogs, magazine covers, books, paraphernalia, and equipment, plus the actual collectable items, if plausible
- Relevant posters (See Resource, #15.)
- Table cover that reflects the theme

Activities
- Have each guest prepare a trivia question for the guest of honor concerning his or her hobby (let the guests know before the party, so they can research the topic, if necessary). Play the trivia game during the party. The guest who stumps the guest of honor gets a prize.
- Play the matching game: Match terminology with the appropriate collection. For example: hinges to stamp collecting, Betty Crocker to cookbook collecting, agate to rock collecting, Morton's and jalapeño to salt-and-pepper-shaker collecting.
- Ask the guest of honor to give a very short talk or demonstration of the pastime.

Refreshments
- Served in any way that complements the theme: food shapes and serving containers related to the theme (giant baseball cards as place mats, postage scale as a serving station, and so on)
- Foods with such names as Postage Potage, Coin-Operated-Machine Coffee, Classic Caramel Corn, Elvis Parsley, Barbie's Bar-B-Que, or Crystal Light

Prizes/Favors
- Souvenir items related to the theme—humorous or functional

For occasions appropriate to this theme, see the theme grid on page 188.

COMPUTERS

A gathering of hacks, nerds, eggheads, and "kings of the on-liners" to compare Net notes and share a byte to eat. Whoever said, "Nothing could be cuter than a person with a computer," must have been to a party like this.

Invitation Ideas
- Write the party information on several continuous sheets of paper (joined by a perforated line). Write the guests' addresses on diskette labels.
- Make small invitations and mail them in diskette mailers.

Dress Options
- Computerese costume—made out of computer paper
- As a computer nerd or a uniformed technician
- As an Apple, a child Prodigy, or one of the yellow Dummies
- Pocket protectors with the guests' names written on them

Decor
- Computer-related posters
- Software packages, keyboards, mice
- Computer-generated banners or posters
- Computer monitors with screen-savers running
- Tablecloth made out of computer paper

Activities
- Have computer game tournaments.
- Set up a chat room (this will have to be explained to computer-illiterates).
- Print out horoscopes, "day you were born" certificates, tarot card readings, or any other computer-generated material. (See Resources, #24.)

Refreshments
- Snacks served on mouse pads and out of diskette holders
- Foods with such names as Hack Snacks, Byte Buffet, and Network Noshes
- Big Macs
- Applesauce, sliced apples, apple pie, or caramel apples

Prizes/Favors
- Replicas of the F3 key, bright-red, and labeled Panic Button (See Resources, #35.)
- Jewelry made with computer chips (easy with glue gun and chips)

For occasions appropriate to this theme, see the theme grid on page 188.

GARDENING

Now here's a bloomin' good theme! To pay tribute to a member of the "green thumb" club, just take a seed of an idea and let it grow. It's actually easier than that, because you will really start with a full-grown idea and make it blossom.

Invitation Ideas
- Decorate the invitations with flowers and leaves.
- Write the party information using such garden-related puns or phrases as "Roses are red, violets are blue...," "Mary, Mary (substitute name of guest of honor) quite contrary, how does your garden grow?"
- Attach seed packets or plant markers to each invitation.
- Make envelopes out of seed-catalog pages or floral paper.

Dress Options
- Floral prints
- As a gardener
- Bedecked with flowers and plants

Decor
- Plants, flowers, tools, misting bottles, pots, gloves, aprons, and bags of soil arranged decoratively on every surface
- Gardening posters, advertising art, photos, paintings, or crafts
- Gardening books and magazines

Activities
- Play the matching game: Match the flower, fruit, or vegetable with the appropriate person, place, or thing. Example: George Washington to cherries, Idaho to potatoes, and so on.
- Hand out song sheets, and sing "flower" songs (for example: "Red Roses for a Blue Lady," "Daisy, Daisy," "You Don't Send Me Flowers Anymore").
- Teach (or hire someone to teach) a crash course in flower arranging.

Refreshments
- Garden-fresh vegetable and fruit dishes of host's choice
- Snacks served in new, clay flower pots, clean seedling trays, or garden-tool carriers
- Beverages served in misting bottles

Prizes/Favors
- Flower seeds, seedlings, and plants
- Gift items with gardening motif: stationery, lotions, sachets, handkerchiefs, jewelry

For occasions appropriate to this theme, see the theme grid on page 188. **119**

GOURMET COOKING

This is a delicious theme whether you actually cook at the party or just design the theme around cooking. For a small group, you can let the guests cook the meal, but when the group is too large for all guests to cook, either let a team do all the cooking, plan a gourmet-only potluck, or hire a caterer.

Invitation Ideas
- Write the party information on large recipe cards, phrasing it to read like a recipe: Combine tasty guests with appealing music; add a heaping spoonful of tempting entertainment and a dash of delicious food. Mix thoroughly for a grand gourmet evening.
- Make envelopes out of magazine pages showing food and wine.
- Enclose a few sprigs of herbs with each invitation.

Dress Options
- Formal or semiformal wear
- As a chef or wine steward

Decor
- Gadgets or containers used in gourmet cooking
- Recipe books and utensils grouped on chopping blocks
- Wine bottles and glasses arranged with flowers and candles
- Wine, food, and gourmet posters

Activities
- Prepare gourmet meals or desserts.
- Wine and dine.
- Play the matching game: Match scrambled, food-related words with their unscrambled mates.
- Have food or wine tasting.

Refreshments
- Gourmet menu, formally served (best china and crystal, waitstaff, music, and so on) (See Resources, #77, 79.)

Prizes/Favors
- Recipes of foods served at the party
- Cooking utensils or gadgets
- Exotic spices or herbs in fancy bottles
- Bottles of wine

For occasions appropriate to this theme, see the theme grid on page 188.

HAYRIDE

Invite your guests to hop aboard a hay wagon for a ride in the country on a sunny day or a star-lit evening. It's good-old-fashioned fun for kids-only, grownups, or the whole family, ending with a warm-up time at the ride site or back at home.

Invitation Ideas
- Attach the invitations to corrugated paper, and decorate with a few pieces of hay.
- Send the invitations in small burlap bags. (See Party How-To's, #3.)

Dress Options
- Ready for the rough-and-tumble action usually experienced on hay-/sleigh rides

Decor
- Strings of lights, bandannas, banners, decorated sawhorses, and hay bales (See Party How-To's, #8.)
- Dining tables draped in checked cloths with kerosene lamps (empty!) and small, decorated hay blocks for centerpieces

Activities
- Square dance.
- Carve pumpkins (if close to Halloween) or make pine bough decorations (if close to Christmas).
- Teach or take straw-crafting lessons.
- Teach or take clogging or line-dancing lessons.
- Bob for apples.

Refreshments
- Warm-up menu of hot toddies, hot cocoa, chili dogs, roasted marshmallows, and hot-fudge sundaes
- Summer specials of icy, cool-down drinks, crisp salads, sandwiches, and an ice-cream sundae bar

Prizes/Favors
- Guests' hand-crafted items
- Instant photos of guests' party activities
- Discount coupons for future rides

For occasions appropriate to this theme, see the theme grid on page 188.

MAKEOVER/MINISPA

This theme is based on relaxation and pampering and can be adapted for birthday parties, graduation parties, baby and wedding showers, and bachelorette blowouts. The guest of honor, and the guests, will be rejuvenated and revivified by the end of this party.

Invitation Ideas
- Attach cotton pads, lotion, cosmetic samples, combs, or emery boards to invitations.
- Make envelopes from magazine ads. (See Resources, #46.)

Dress Options
- Bathrobes (guests can bring them to the party, to be comfortable)
- Thong shoes, to wear after a pedicure

Decor
- Towels spread on couches
- Humidifiers running in various corners of the room
- Footbaths set out for the guests
- Beauty supplies set out around the room.
- Soft nature sounds or new-age music
- Scented candles

Activities
- Have the guests give themselves or each other facials, manicures, massages, hair treatments, and experimental makeup applications.
- Organize a professional massage for the guest of honor.
- Take silly before and after instant photos.

Refreshments
- Mineral water and juices
- Salads, fresh fruits, and vegetables

Prizes/Favors
- A goody bag of pampering essentials in sample sizes
- Discount coupons for salons or beauty supply stores
- Nail polish supplies
- Travel-sized beauty supplies

For occasions appropriate to this theme, see the theme grid on page 188.

MUSIC

A music lovers' party is as easy to plan as falling off a piano stool, because theme-related items are everywhere. Party paraphernalia for one who loves music is readily available, although supplies for specific areas of music, such as classical, country western, or jazz, will pose more of a challenge.

Invitation Ideas
- Write the party information on pages of sheet music.
- Format the invitations to look like album covers, featuring the guest of honor as the artist.
- Write the party information on CD labels, and send them in diskette mailers.

Dress Options
- Formal or casual wear, host's choice
- As a famous musician, in the theme
- As a famous music title, in the theme

Decor
- Music posters and photos
- Sheet music, album covers, musical instruments
- Large paper or cardboard cutouts of music notes, clefs, and instruments
- Table cover made out of white paper and decorated with music notes
- Small instrument cases for decorative table arrangements

Activities
- Listen, sing, and dance to music.
- Play Name That Tune or music trivia games.
- Play the matching game: Match artists to songs or composers to musical works.
- Sing karaoke.
- Give a concert with kazoos and homemade instruments.

Refreshments
- Host's choice buffet, served on black-and-white paper or plastic products

Prizes/Favors
- Note pads, Post-It Notes
- Magnets of musical instruments and music notes (See Resources, #8.)
- Tapes and records, vintage or contemporary
- Concert tickets
- Audiotapes of karaoke performances

For occasions appropriate to this theme, see the theme grid on page 188. **123**

NIGHT AT THE . . .
(THEATER, BALLET, OR OPERA)

Those who appreciate the theater, ballet, or opera will love a party based upon any and all of the three. If you plan to take your guests to a performance that will take up most of the evening, plans for decor and activities are minimized. Otherwise, design your party incorporating details from one or all three events.

Invitation Ideas
- Format the invitations to look and read like playbills or theater tickets.
- Tuck each invitation inside a white glove, and give the other glove at the party.
- Make the envelopes out of magazine pages or gift wrap that follows the party theme.
- Record an RSVP voice-mail message with appropriate background music.

Dress Options
- Formal
- As a character from a play, opera, or ballet
- As a theater usher or backstage crew person

Decor
- Posters and playbills from performances
- Seating arranged for an audience
- Costumes and props related to the theme
- Small stage set up for miniperformances or photos
- Stage backdrop with the guest-of-honor's name or face incorporated into the design

Activities
- Watch a short performance. (Invite a local theater group.)
- Stage a performance, with costumes and props.
- Take instant souvenir photos on the stage.

Refreshments
- Preperformance: Appetizers and light beverages
- Postperformance: Late-night supper
- Nonperformance: All of the above, served either as a buffet or a sit-down dinner, depending on the number of guests

Prizes/Favors
- Gifts, stationery, or gadgets appropriate to the party theme
- Tickets or passes to performances
- Opera glasses (real or gag)
- White glove

For occasions appropriate to this theme, see the theme grid on page 188.

PETS

Since most people either have or have had a pet at some time in their lives, this party theme has universal appeal. And the guest of honor will be pleased and flattered when you pay tribute to his or her canine or feline "kids."

Invitation Ideas
- Decorate the invitations with paw-print graphics, sketches of pets, or photos of the guest of honor with pet(s).
- Enclose a pet snack or a pet-food sample with each invitation.
- Record an RSVP voice-mail message with pet sounds in the background.

Dress Options
- As a pet
- As a "gone overboard" pet owner
- Host's choice

Decor
- Pet movie or book posters, photos, product advertisements
- Pet paraphernalia: beds, collars, leashes, toys, brushes, food packages (No litter boxes, please!)
- Stuffed or papier-mâché animals in all sizes

Activities
- Declare pet peeves, and award a prize for the funniest.
- Play the matching game: Match famous persons to their pets (for example: the Flintstones to Dino).
- Have a songfest of pet-lovers songs (for example: "Puppy Love," "Alley Cat," "What's New, Pussycat," and "How Much Is That Doggy in the Window?").

Refreshments
- Snacks served in new, washed pet bowls
- Foods with such names as Fido's Favorites, Bowzer's Burgers, Kitty's Klassics, Puppy Chow Mein, Rovers Refills, Vets Vittles, or Meow, Meow Menu

Prizes/Favors
- Stationery, gifts, or trinkets with the appropriate pet theme
- Books, magazines, and videos with a pet theme

For occasions appropriate to this theme, see the theme grid on page 188.

PHOTOGRAPHY

When you throw a party for your favorite shutter bug, go wild with "photo" stuff; something wonderful is sure to develop. Of course, the most important part of the planning is to line up a good photographer to document the party, since the guest of honor is off duty.

Invitation Ideas
- Write the party information on a poster, and take a very clear photo of the poster. Make as many copies as you need and use them as invitations.
- Send the invitations in photo-processing envelopes (put the address labels on the front).

Dress Options
- As a photographer or a person from a famous photograph
- Loaded with cameras and camera equipment

Decor
- Photos, camera equipment, and equipment packaging
- Film posters and magazine covers
- Lighting, backdrop, reflectors, and props arranged for guest photo sessions
- Expired film (check photo labs or shops) strung around the buffet table
- Photographs in individual or collage frames
- A tablecloth made out of photographers' backdrop paper or fabric
- Napkin holders made out of empty film boxes or film (cut film into strips, form a ring, and glue the ends of the ring together)

Activities
- Photograph continuously: instant photos for immediate enjoyment, and regular film to be developed later.
- Present a slide show of humorous photos of the guest of honor. (Request these photos from the guests in the invitations.)
- Award prizes for funniest photos.
- Play a pencil-and-paper game: Have guests write down words using the letters in the word "photography." The guest who lists the most words wins.

Refreshments
- Menu of host's choice
- Snacks and foods served from camera- or photo-equipment packaging

Prizes/Favors
- Gifts in tiny film containers: scarves, jewelry, magnets, herbs, bath salts, lotions
- Photo frames
- Instant-photos of guests
- Single-use cameras

TOOLS/WORKSHOP

If you are planning a celebration for a person who has a passion for tools, woodworking, or home improvements, this blueprint is pretty easy to follow. And for more ideas on this theme, just stand in the middle of the guest-of-honor's workshop.

Invitation Ideas
- Tie each invitation around a small screwdriver or wrench.
- Glue a few wood shavings to each invitation.

Dress Options
- Workshop wardrobe
- As "Al" on the TV show *Home Improvement*: plaid shirt, jeans
- Tool belt, hard hat, boots, and goggles

Decor
- Buffet table made of two sawhorses and planks
- Blueprints or project plans covering tables and hanging on walls
- Huge, inflatable hammers
- Saw (new or cleaned) laying next to the cake, as a spoof for cutting
- Hardware and tool displays and posters
- Tool chest filled with brown paper nail bags that contain flatware and napkins (no nails!)
- Centerpieces made of wood shavings glued to small sticks of wood and arranged in a work boot or nail box

Note: If you have children at this party, don't leave tools (such as the saw) within reach.

Activities
- Play the matching game: Write jumbled versions of tool names on pieces of paper and give them out to guests. Then have the guests figure out the name of the tool and find the matching tool. (Be sure to have all corresponding tools as part of the decor.)
- Sing a parody of "If I Had a Hammer." (See Resources, #25.)

Refreshments
- Snacks served from (clean!) hard hats and tool carriers
- Foods with such names as Hammerburgers, Wrench Dressing, Knot Hole Donuts, Nuts without Bolts
- Such drinks as Screwdrivers, Harvey Wall Bangers, and Rusty Nails

Prizes/Favors
- Miniature tool sets
- TV show *Home Improvement* memorabilia

For occasions appropriate to this theme, see the theme grid on page 188.

TRAVEL

If your guest of honor has a favorite spot on the globe, that will streamline your plans. But if he or she just loves to travel any- and everywhere, you will have a sea of theme possibilities. Take your guests for a sail, a flight, a ride, or a drive to an imaginary destination of any town, state, or country in the world.

Invitation Ideas
- Tuck each invitation into a travel brochure, or glue each one onto a map section.
- Format the invitations to look and read like passports or airline tickets, and attach a baggage tag to each one.
- Decorate the envelopes with travel stickers.
- Record an RSVP voice-mail message with transportation sounds (train whistle, airplane roar, road sounds, or boat whistle) in the background.

Dress Options
- As tourists or as natives of a favorite destination
- As a ticket or travel agent, or as a uniformed travel employee

Decor
- Travel posters, magazine covers, and travel advertising
- Suitcases, travel bags, trunks, luggage carts
- Travel/ticket counter (to serve as a bar)
- Departures and arrivals chart hanging behind the bar

Activities
- Play the matching game: Match state or country to its capital city.
- Hand out song sheets and sing "travel destination" songs (for example: "Jet Plane," "Chattanooga Choo Choo," "Slow Boat to China").
- Threaten to show travel slides—set up slide equipment with a huge stack of slide containers to put a real scare into the guests.

Refreshments
- Food served at bus stops (doughnuts, coffee, sandwiches), in dining cars (standard fare served in restaurants), or on airplanes (on small trays, in small portions)
- Foods and beverages representative of favorite destinations
- Potluck menu, with guests bringing food that represents their travels
- Snacks in miniature luggage and baskets, labeled with baggage claim tickets

Prizes/Favors
- Travel-sized toiletry kits: soap, shampoo, lotion, shower cap, toothbrush carriers
- Souvenirs from the guest-of-honor's favorite trip or ideal destination (Travel agencies may be good resources, but these favors may require searching and planning.)
- Instant photos of guests in travel settings

For occasions appropriate to this theme, see the theme grid on page 188.

BOWLING

Whether you actually take your party bowling, your party will be all about bowling. You will make a perfect score when you use this theme for your favorite King Pin Kegler.

Invitation Ideas
- Use bowling score sheets for the invitations and envelopes.

Dress Options
- Bowling shirts and shoes, but casual shirts and slacks will do
- Self-adhesive name patches (Ralph's Alley Pal or Johnson's Team) for guests to wear on their bowling shirts

Decor
- Bowling pins (cleaned up or spray-painted) for table decorations
- Posters and advertising art from bowling allies
- Bowling ball with flowers poking out of finger holes for buffet table
- Score-sheet place mats
- Trophies, trophies, and more trophies (use trophy cups to hold snacks)
- *Honeymooners* posters and memorabilia scattered around the room
- Black lunch pails and plungers to pay tribute to Ralph Kramden and Ed Norton

Activities
- Go bowling or set up a makeshift lane in your basement or backyard for guests who can't control themselves when they wear bowling shoes.
- Stage a Ralph and Alice Kramden and Ed and Trixie Norton look-alike contest.
- Play a Bowlerama Trivia Game: Names, titles, or phrases that contain the word "bowl."

Refreshments
- A sandwich bar, with sandwich names such as The Lois Lane, The Nathan Lane, The Shirley McLaine, The Alley McGraw, The Kristie Alley, The Mohammed Alley
- "Spare" ribs
- Banana splits
- Beer in the bottle

Prizes/Favors
- Small bowling-pin key chains
- *Honeymooners* videos
- Small trophies
- Bowling-alley passes

For occasions appropriate to this theme, see the theme grid on page 188. **129**

GOLF/TENNIS

Golf and tennis parties are ideal theme parties for enthusiasts of any gender. Although guests will not actually play either sport at the party, the decorations, refreshments, and activities are all designed to follow the theme.

Invitation Ideas
- Decorate invitations with stickers or rubber-stamp art.
- For golf: Attach invitations to related items, such as golf tees and scorecards with small pencils.
- For tennis: Attach invitations to terry wristbands or minirackets.

Dress Options
- Uniform for the designated sport

Decor
- Standard party decor, such as balloons and streamers
- Posters and advertising displays solicited from your local club or sports-equipment store
- Equipment such as golf balls, bags, clubs, ball buckets/tennis rackets, nets (If using discarded equipment, spray the equipment with gold or silver paint to create an elegant atmosphere for a more formal dinner party.)
- For golf: AstroTurf on the cake table, small flags marking the foods, snack containers made from golf-ball boxes and buckets, serving utensils wrapped with terry cloth fingertip towels, especially at casual affairs

Activities
- Set up a miniature putting green, and give prize tickets for shots under par.
- Organize minitournaments with table tennis.
- Play the matching game: Match scrambled words with the item. For example: Write "ctakre" on a piece of paper or board, and the guests have to find a racket to claim a prize. (Be sure items matching the scrambled word are in the room.)

Refreshments
- For tennis: Foods and beverages with such names as Lobbers Lobster, Netty Nuts, Racket Rolls, Love 'n' Quiches, Backhand Burgers, Center Court Cocktails, and Davis Cupful
- For golf: Foods and beverages with such names as Chip Shots & Dip, Salad Greens, Country Club Sandwiches, Birdie Burgers, Divot Divine Dessert, Hole-in-One Donuts, Coffee á la Cart, Long Island Tee

Prizes/Favors
- Any trinkets, books, games, stationery, or jewelry relating to the theme
- Picture frames in the shapes of sports balls
- Passes for courses or courts

 For occasions appropriate to this theme, see the theme grid on page 188.

HEALTH AND FITNESS

Plan this robust and healthy party for either a "health-nut" or a "keep-in-shape" devotee. The result will be an energetic, invigorating, and entertaining event.

Invitation Ideas
- Roll invitations inside terry wristbands or headbands.
- Embroider or paint the guest-of-honor's name and the party date on the bands.

Dress Options
- Exercise sweats or dance gear (but comfortable, casual wear will be fine also)

Decor
- Health and nutrition posters
- Exercise equipment
- A marathon banner with the guest-of-honor's name
- Fitness and health magazine covers plastered around the room
- Fresh flowers, plants, and herbs in pots

Activities
- Play a rousing blast of aerobics music to greet guests.
- Conduct a minisession of calisthenics.
- Take a brisk walk around the block.
- Dance to videos for aerobics pros.
- Watch videos, without participating.

Note: If you are using this theme for a coed baby shower, have your guests do "labor-intensive" breathing exercises.

Refreshments
- Healthy, delicious, and beautiful food
- Blender "smoothie" drinks
- Whole-grain baked goodies
- Fat-free foods
- Fresh fruits and vegetables
- Yogurt desserts

Prizes/Favors
- Visors, hats, and T-shirts
- Exercise books, videos, and tapes
- Health-food samples
- Water bottles

For occasions appropriate to this theme, see the theme grid on page 188.

HUNTING/FISHING

Although you won't actually be out in the woods or on a lake for this party, by creating an "as if" situation with decor and dress, you'll find that planning an event for a favorite "lover of the outdoors" will be as much fun as "landing the big one."

Invitation Ideas
- Attach invitations to fishing lures (de-hooked) or to bright orange shoestrings.
- Send invitations with brochures or postcards from fishing/hunting resorts.
- Enclose hunting/fishing license name tags with the invitations.

Dress Options
- Outfit appropriate for the chosen sport

Decor
- Fishing or hunting gear of every description hanging on walls and over windows and doorways, and spread out on tables, shelves, and counters
- Hats, buckets, or baskets used as serving containers
- Fishing or hunting posters, advertising art, maps, and photos displayed on walls
- Duck decoys or fish floating in pool and bathtubs
- Camouflage fabric or fish netting as table covers
- Centerpieces made of inverted hats with woodsy or lakefront greens and flowers

Activities
For fishing:
- Play a fish pond game, with guests angling for prizes.
- Have a lure-tying demonstration.
- Conduct fish-cleaning lessons (make the lesson into a spoof, with soap, brush, battery-operated face scrubber, and so on).
- Take photos with a Fish-Holding-Person photo front. (See Party How-To's, #6.)
For hunting:
- Play "Knocking ducks off a shelf with a slingshot" game.
- Have a duck call concert.
- Play a lively game of Duck, Duck, Gray Duck.
- Give out awards for Best Costume, for both themes.

Refreshments
- Fish fry or hunt feast (venison, duck, pheasant, game hens)
- Beer with theme-appropriate names, such as Stag Head

Prizes/Favors
- Fishing lure jewelry or trinkets
- Duck calls or fine-feathered gift items
- Rubber duckies painted to look like decoys

For occasions appropriate to this theme, see the theme grid on page 188.

ICE/ROLLER SKATING

When paying tribute to someone who has a real passion for skating on ice, wood, or pavement, you may or may not be able to include the activity in your party plan. However, this theme has so many entertaining and amusing facets, your party will roll right along to a successful finale.

Invitation Ideas
- For ice skating: Write the words "We'll All Have an 'Ice' Time" on a piece of Mylar paper with fake snowflakes glued to a Mylar "pond."
- For roller skating: Cut out a roller skate from a 5-by-7-inch cardstock; secure the wheels with metal paper fasteners to allow them to turn.

Dress Options
- Typical garb for skating activities

Decor
- Posters, advertising art, and photos of skaters
- Clean skating gear (new, if used near food), arranged creatively
- Mirrors on table to simulate ice, with fake snow sprinkles
- Skates filled with arrangements of flowers or frosted branches

Activities
- Do the activity, if possible.
- View home videos or skating competitions.

Note: In some areas you can arrange to have an in-line skating company come out to your party site with a van filled with skates. Check with your sports equipment store or the *Yellow Pages*.

Refreshments
- For ice skating: Warm-up foods, such as chili, stew, hot sandwiches, and hot beverages
- For roller skating: Chilled salads, cold-cut buffet, fruit and vegetable trays, icy beverages in water bottles

Note: If not going skating, any menu works.

Prizes/Favors
- Trinkets or gift items relating to the theme
- Ear muffs or visors
- Thermos or water bottles
- Skating passes

KITE FLYING

Keep your fingers crossed for a great day, then gather at an open field with kites for all your guests. Be sure to have an "in-case-of-rain" plan to take the party indoors for some spirited and creative fun, including making kites to be enjoyed on the next breezy day.

Invitation Ideas
- Make small kites out of tissue paper and Popsicle sticks. Write the party information on the tissue paper or on separate pieces of paper, which you can attach to the kites as tails.
- Use kids' kindergarten-style drawings of kites as invitations, with real string tails attached.
- Send the invitations rolled up in tubes. (See Resources, #29.)

Dress Options
- Casual, loose, and comfortable "kite-flying gear" and "fleet-of-foot wear" to help runners keep up with the billowing kites

Decor
- Kites of all manner (indoor or outdoor), all ready for guests to set afloat
- Picnic tables and serving surfaces covered with bright fabrics
- Coordinating serving ware, plastic or paper
- Decorated auto and truck tailgates with kite tails, balloons, and streamers
- Blankets spread on the ground for picnics

Activities
- Make and fly kites.
- Play horseshoes and badminton.
- Conduct a variety of activity races.

Refreshments
- Potluck, picnic fare
- Lots of thirst-quenching beverages

Prizes/Favors
- Unique kite varieties
- Books about kites and kite making
- Gimmick kite gift items
- Instant photos of guests in full kite-flying mode

 For occasions appropriate to this theme, see the theme grid on page 188.

SKIING/SLEDDING/ SLEIGHING

With the proper atmosphere, you can create a "winter sport" theme party any time of the year. For example, if your guest of honor has a birthday in July and has a passion for skiing, planning a Sizzling on the Slopes party can be a down-hill breeze. Of course, a wintertime party will be "cool" too.

Invitation Ideas
- Glue "faux flakes" all over the invitations.
- Send invitations in envelopes with see-through pockets filled with flakes. (See Resources, #29.)
- Write the party information on ski-lift tags, and attach tags to mittens; mail in padded envelopes.

Dress Options
- Appropriate for the sport

Decor
- Travel posters, photos, and advertising art
- Winter sports equipment and apparel

Activities
- Do the actual activity, if possible.
- Watch videos or telecasts of events.
- Play board games or charades.

Refreshments
- Defrosting delights, such as mulled cider, hot cocoa, coffee, tea, and toddies
- Snowball cupcakes, baked Alaska, and Eskimo Pies
- Cold drinks served from an Igloo container

Prizes/Favors
- The other mitten (to match the invitation mitten)
- Ear muffs, mufflers
- Passes or admissions to sports events or recreational areas

For occasions appropriate to this theme, see the theme grid on page 188.   **135**

WINTER AND SUMMER OLYMPICS/ATHLETICS

Here's another "watch it or do it" theme. You can produce an Olympic-theme event any time of the year, but if you want your party to coincide with the actual Olympics, schedule it in February or July. An Olympic-watching theme party can have activities that test the physical and mental skills of guests, aged one to 100, during intermissions of televised competitions.

Invitation Ideas
- Fold card cutouts in the shape of gold medals, write party information on the inside flaps, and list the scheduled events on the backs.
- Make invitations to look like newsclippings, with photos of the guest of honor featured as a gold medal winner.
- Send the invitations in gold envelopes with Olympic-symbol seals.

Dress Options
- Casual, comfortable clothing
- Specific event uniforms
- National team colors
- Costumes of press corps members

Decor
- Banners, posters, and signs—authentic or replicas
- Sports equipment and uniforms—hanging, draped, or utilized as containers
- Posters of event time schedules

Activities
- Watch events on television.
- Organize teams for relays and races.
- Write trivia questions on slips of paper and post them around the party room. Have guests write answers along with their names on separate slips of paper and drop the slips into a container for a prize drawing.
- Ask trivia questions for mental Olympics (during TV watching).
- Award prizes to winners of all events.

Refreshments
- Typical sports-event menu: hot dogs, hamburgers, coleslaw, potato chips, popcorn, pretzels, ice-cream treats, cookies, beer, sports drinks, and soda pop
- International favorites to salute other teams

Prizes/Favors
- Instant photos of guests next to sports-celebrity cardboard standup (See Resources, #1.)
- Authentic souvenirs from Olympics or Special Olympics
- Sports medals and ribbons

ACADEMY AWARDS

Roll out the red carpet to welcome your guests as they arrive to watch the gala that brings out the who's who of the film industry. This party provides a good excuse to dress up and rub elbows with your own stars.

Invitation Ideas
- Use formal invitations. Write "The Envelope Please" on the envelopes.
- Enclose an RSVP card designed to look like a voting ballot, including the names of the nominees in each category (nominate each guest in an award category appropriate to his or her personality or occupation).

Dress Options
- Formal attire, contemporary or vintage (See Resources, #70.)
- Costumes appropriate for a role in one of the nominated films

Decor
- Red carpet on walkway or hallway
- Lights (you can use heavy-duty flashlights pointing toward the ceiling)
- Hollywood movie posters on the walls (See Resources, #10.)
- Papier-mâché statuettes displayed on the awards table (sprayed or painted gold, if possible)
- Life-sized, standup cutouts of movie greats, used as official greeters (See Resources, #1.)
- Auditorium or dining table seating
- Movie clapboards, stars, and tinsel for table decor
- Podium for the awards ceremony

Activities
- Have some of the guests act as paparazzi, taking tabloid photos throughout the party (or hire a photographer).
- Play movie trivia games.
- Videotape guests' predictions for winners, and replay after the awards.
- Give out awards for outstanding costumes.

Refreshments
- Elegant snacks and beverages befitting a room full of movie moguls and stars, passed on silver trays by formally attired servers (that means white gloves)
- Champagne fountain (full champagne glasses stacked into a pyramid)

Prizes/Favors
- Instant photos of guests with standup cutouts or live look-alikes
- Large photos of classic movie stars
- Movie passes
- Videos of movie classics

For occasions appropriate to this theme, see the theme grid on page 188.   **137**

ELECTION RETURNS

The first Tuesday after the first Monday in November marks election day. Watching the election returns with friends is a fine time to catch up on conversation, since the program will usually have plenty of lulls to fill. You might want to have at least two television viewing areas, to make sure both sides can watch the coverage they prefer.

Invitation Ideas
- Trim your red, white, and blue invitations with U.S. flag toothpicks. (See Resources, #7.)
- Attach a paper chef's hat (personalized with guest's name), streamers, and a noise maker to each invitation. Write "You're Invited to a Pizza and Polling Party" on the invitation. Send everything in a small pizza box.
- Design your invitations to look like bumper stickers by writing the party information on a piece of self-adhesive paper.

Dress Options
- Red, white, and blue clothing and straw hats with patriotic bands
- Personalized pizza chef's hats

Decor
- Red, white, and blue bunting
- Balloons and streamers
- Candidates' posters, flags, voting registration advertisements, ballots strung on stings, and election-day banners

Activities
- Play political trivia games.
- Play Pin the Tail on the Donkey, and Pin the Trunk on the Elephant.
- Vote for "best dressed," "nicest smile," "straightest teeth," "wildest tie," "best handshake," and other silly titles.
- Celebrate or commiserate when returns are all in.
- Dance and sing along to "Happy Days Are Here Again," "It's a Grand Old Flag," and "Yankee Doodle Dandy." (See Resources, #80.)

Refreshments
- Pizza made with your guests' favorite toppings
- Foods with such names as Election Elixirs, Voters Veggies, Political Pastries
- Campaign Champagne

Prizes/Favors
- Donkey and elephant key chains and refrigerator magnets
- Small trophies or badges for winners of "Best" elections
- Pizza discount coupons

For occasions appropriate to this theme, see the theme grid on page 188.

EMMY AWARDS

The Emmies reward and award the television industry. This show is as glittery and show-bizzy as the Oscars, and it gives us another great excuse to throw a party. Guests—couch potatoes or not—enjoy watching television to find out what people are watching on television!

Invitation Ideas
- Attach a group photo of guests to a *TV Guide* cover with the caption: "Top TV Talent Gets Tallied." On the other side (or inside, if folded), write the party information as a TV schedule.
- Wrap the invitations in plain brown-paper sleeve-mailers.

Dress Options
- Costumes of favorite TV characters, especially Emmy nominees
- Outfits representing popular TV commercials
- Formal wear—glamour, glitter, and glitz

Decor
- Many TV sets—grouped in one place or spread throughout the party room(s)
- Old or broken TV sets used as serving stations or as awards (garage sales are a great source for cheap TV sets)
- *TV Guide* covers, superimposed with photos of the guest of honor and other guests, blown up to poster size
- Sets from famous TV shows
- Rabbit ear charms sprayed gold or wrapped in aluminum foil, trimmed with decorative stars (can also be used as awards)
- Serving stations designed as food commercials

Activities
- Videotape celebrity entrances.
- Watch the awards; draw ballots for the winners.
- Act-out short scripts.
- Set up a talk show set, and videotape interviews; watch the videos during dessert.
- Play TV Trivia. (See Resources, #81.)
- Present awards to the guest nominee winners.

Refreshments
- Snack food and dinner, if served, spread out on TV trays

Prizes/Favors
- A potato sprayed with gold paint (an award created for the event)
- Instant photos with celebrities (cutouts or look-alikes)
- Remote-control holders
- TV trivia games

For occasions appropriate to this theme, see the theme grid on page 188.

GRAMMY AWARDS

Hear the top recordings of the year, and witness the artists accepting their coveted statuettes—another excellent reason to plan a party based upon celebrity watching at its best.

Invitation Ideas
- Write the invitations on the labels of 45 records or, to be current, on shiny CDs (obtained from a radio deejay who receives hundreds each month).
- Send the invitations in padded envelopes or CD mailers.
- Record the party information on an audio cassette, and record a matching RSVP voice-mail message. (See Resources, #25.)

Dress Options
- "To the nines" for a gala night out
- As a recording artist, especially one who is nominated for a Grammy

Decor
- Record album covers, posters, photos of artists
- CDs, 45s, LPs—dangling artistically from the ceiling
- Sheet music, *Billboard Magazine* covers
- Various paraphernalia for a minirecording studio (earphones, microphones, red "recording" light)—can be used for karaoke singing during the party
- Red carpet for arrivals
- Inflatable musical instruments
- Grammy replicas
- Black tablecloth accessorized with musical motif
- Old LP album covers, for hot pads or decorative mats

Activities
- Greet the arrivals with paparazzi flashes.
- Vote for nominees of choice.
- Play Grammy winners trivia quiz.
- Sing karaoke during commercial breaks. (See Resources, #33.)
- Award prizes to top quiz scorers and singers.
- Play the matching game: Match artists to song titles.

Refreshments
- Backstage buffet, with snacks and junk food for hungry stars
- Beverages with such names as Tequila Sunrise, Wine Spolioli, 100 Bottles of Beer, Tiny Bubbles, and so on

Prizes/Favors
- Tapes, CDs, MTV videos
- Cassette tapes of karaoke stars
- Instant photos of your Grammy guests

For occasions appropriate to this theme, see the theme grid on page 188.

INDY 500

Rally 'round the flag—checkered flag that is—for an event planned around viewing the biggest national auto race of the year. Pick a favorite car, and root its driver over the finish line. Pit stops for refreshments and socializing are plentiful at this party.

Invitation Ideas
- Decorate the invitations with checkered flags and automobile logos.
- Design the invitations to look and read as racing flyers.
- Enclose a tiny auto race car with each invitation; send in padded envelopes.

Dress Options
- Racing colors, jumpsuits
- As a "fan in the stands"

Decor
- All-American red, white, and blue color scheme
- Race flags and event promotional posters (See Resources, #9.)
- Checkered tablecloths, theme serving ware and paper products
- Stacks of tires used as table bases, waste receptacles, or a huge ice bucket
- Photos of racing celebrities (to be identified during the party as an activity)
- Trophies and racing paraphernalia
- Mobiles of auto-product logos and fake money
- Auto-race sound effects and "Back Home in Indiana" playing in the background
- Food area labeled Gasoline Alley Pit Stop

Activities
- Have miniraces with battery-operated, radio-controlled Indy race cars.
- Wager on race winners and times.
- Organize teams and have them unscramble brand names of automobiles, and/or have them match brand names with advertising slogans.
- Watch the race or selected taped moments.

Refreshments
- Grandstand concession foods served in cardboard containers: hot dogs, burgers, corn on the cob
- Milk straight out of the quart bottle—the winner's drink
- Beer by the bottle or keg
- Foods with such names as Andretti's Spaghetti, Mears' Beers, Lola Cola, Goodyear Goodies

Prizes/Favors
- Checkered bandannas
- Logo hats, T-shirts, and bags
- "Clippin' Along" Minicar Favor (See Party How-To's, #15.)

For occasions appropriate to this theme, see the theme grid on page 188.

KENTUCKY DERBY

Since the first race in 1875, the greatest thoroughbred horses "Run for the Roses" on the first Saturday in May. The Derby has been celebrated most vigorously at its home site in Louisville, Kentucky. But wherever you gather—at Churchill Downs, in South Philly, or in Southern California—your enthusiastic party-goers will be off and running.

Invitation Ideas
- Paint plastic horseshoes with gold paint and attach them to the invitations.
- Send the invitations in padded envelopes marked "Sent by Pony Express."

Dress Options
- Formal: tails and top hats for gents, and organdy frocks and huge picture hats for ladies
- Casual, backyard wear, horsing around attire

Decor
- Real, paper, plastic, or silk roses everywhere
- Photos, drawings, or paintings of winning horses
- Posters or signs from travel agencies
- Betting cage
- Racing silks and jockey's hats
- Horse-related equipment, such as bridles, harnesses, blankets, oats buckets, and gold horseshoes (See Resources, #5.)

Activities
- Assign each guest or team a Derby entrant's name.
- Give play money for making wagers at the betting cage.
- Watch the race on TV.
- Play horseshoes.
- Take instant photos of guests on a "sawhorse" nag.
- Play horseplay trivia game: books, songs, products, movies, television shows, and people's names that contain the word "horse" or other horse-related terms.
- Present the winning "horse" a wreath of carrots, greens, and wilted roses.

Refreshments
- Frosty Mint Juleps, in glasses or cups
- Mint tea with strawberries and fresh cream
- Snacks served in inverted derby hats
- Horseradish served on the side or mixed in to spice up any dish

Prizes/Favors
- Books, tapes, videos about Black Beauty, Flicka, Dan Patch, Sea Biscuit, Mr. Ed
- Real horseshoes for good luck

For occasions appropriate to this theme, see the theme grid on page 188.

NBA FINALS/
NCAA FINAL FOUR

Just another excuse to get looped! Oops, I mean, hooped! The action on the court will keep the hoop-a-holic guests mesmerized, while other bits of activity will keep less-than-avid fans hoopy—I mean, happy! (Sometimes, I just can't help myself.)

Invitation Ideas
- Mat the invitations on pages from newspaper or magazine sports' pages, and make the envelopes out of such pages also.
- Enclose a customized basketball trading card with each invitation. (See Resources, #16.)
- Enclose a player's number your guests can wear on their T-shirts.

Dress Options
- As player, coach, referee, fan, or member of the press

Decor
- "Nerf"-type hoops attached to doors in every room
- Posters, garments, team memorabilia
- Poster with photo of guest-of-honor's face superimposed over that of a sports star (leave enough border blank for guests to write greetings)

Activities
- Guess the winning team.
- Have guests try "free throws" to earn points. With the points, they can "buy" entry slips for a prize drawing.
- Provide nongame watchers with household items, kitchen utensils, and art supplies, and have them prepare a halftime show.
- Take photos with "Magic" or "Shaq" cardboard standup photos. (See Resources, #1.)

Refreshments
- Various game-watching munchies
- Foods with such names as Lakers Liquor, Knicks Knoshes, Pistons Pizza
- Slam-dunkin' doughnuts

Prizes/Favors
- Gift "baskets" of relaxation items for couples: massage oils and creams, bath salts, loofah sponges, herbal teas
- Basketball trivia games, souvenirs, books, or videos for fans

For occasions appropriate to this theme, see the theme grid on page 188.

SOAP OPERA AWARDS

Who has more fun: the soap opera fans or the guests who spoof the soap opera fans? Everyone has loads of fun at this event that features good, clean people-watching. As a soap fan never misses an episode, your guests won't miss your party.

Invitation Ideas
- Write the party information on formal cards, and attach them to small bars of soap.
- Tuck the invitations inside small packs of tissues, for the sob-sessions.
- Tape a soap-opera-like RSVP message on your voice mail. For example: "Will you be coming to our party? Will the chip find romance with dip? Will the host stay awake till the end? For the answers to these and many more questions, please say 'yes' at the tone."

Dress Options
- As a favorite soap star or soap opera fan

Decor
- Posters, advertising art, product packaging
- Blowups of star photos displayed with guests' photos
- Lavish soap opera-ish settings
- Flower arrangements in detergent boxes
- Signs: General Hospitality (on the front door), The Guiding Light Switch, Another World (on bedroom door), Days of Our Lives (over the calendar)

Activities
- Vote for winners.
- Stage and videotape short soap opera vignettes (set up a filming area, assign a director to help guests act out short scripts, and appoint a MAKEUP! artist with a big powder puff).
- Watch the resulting videos.
- Award prizes for the best video.
- Record (ahead of time) theme soap music, and play Name That Soap Theme.

Refreshments
- All beverages served in champagne glasses
- Snacks served from facial tissue boxes
- Foods labeled The Hot and the Spicy, The Sweet and the Gooey, The Rich and the Fattening, The Frosty and the Frigid, All My Chocolate

Prizes/Favors
- Copies of video performances
- Decorative tissue-box covers
- Bubble bath bottles
- Fancy soaps

For occasions appropriate to this theme, see the theme grid on page 188.

SUPER BOWL

This one will bowl you over! Guests show up representing a famous bowl—whether associated with a sporting event or a whimsical idea, such as the "Salad Bowl" or "Fish Bowl." Add fun-foolery to the prime TV-football-watching day of the year.

Invitation Ideas
- Print the party information on round pieces of paper; fit the circles into the bottoms of small, disposable plastic bowls; add a few chips or pieces of popcorn for a preparty snack; shrink-wrap the bowls with sturdy plastic wrap; attach labels and postage to the outside; mail.
- Design the invitations as coveted Super Bowl tickets, with the party information incorporated into ticket data.

Dress Options
- Authentic football gear
- Cheer-ful costumes
- Costume to represent your "bowl of choice"

Decor
- Furniture draped with blankets, sheets, spreads, and draperies with a football insignia pattern
- Posters, clothing, sports equipment, and team pennants hanging on the walls, ceiling, and so on
- AstroTurf lining the entrance or front walk
- A concession stand dispensing gourmet game goodies
- AstroTurf-covered table; napkins hanging over a goalpost at the end of the table

Activities
- Wager in a football pool.
- Play football trivia at halftime.
- Have guests who are not big football fans rehearse and perform an impromptu halftime show with corny cheers and nonsynchronized dancing.
- Award prizes for most-original "bowl" concept.

Refreshments
- Favorite game-day fare dispensed by stadium hawkers from waist-high trays
- Ball-game buffet served in helmets, shoulder pads, and other theme-related containers

Prizes/Favors
- Football motif magnets, pens, key chains, photo frames
- Football wearables: hats, T-shirts, visors
- Books, videos, magazines, sports cards

For occasions appropriate to this theme, see the theme grid on page 188.

WORLD SERIES

Even nonfans of baseball "get up" for the last game of the series. Since the date of the last game can't be guaranteed, the party has to be impromptu. You can be prepared with elaborate plans, though, especially if the game falls on a weekend night.

Invitation Ideas
- Leave the "When" blank on your invitations or write "Final Game Night."
- Print the invitations on paper pennants.
- Write the party information on balloons: Inflate white balloons; draw baseball stitching in black; write your information in red. Deflate and send.
- Make the envelopes from the paper used to wrap hot dogs.

Dress Options
- Favorite team colors
- As mascots, umpires, or food vendors

Decor
- Posters, pennants, streamers, baseball-card mobiles, promotional items
- Bleachers or chairs arranged to simulate bleachers
- A backdrop mural of a crowd scene placed behind the TV
- Flower arrangements in baseball shoes
- Baseball cards glued to ponytail holders for napkin rings
- Tablecloth made out of sports magazine pages

Activities
- Write the name of a player on each guest's name tag (there might be repeats), so the crowd can cheer or jeer for players. Make a "goat" hat to be passed around as needed, for the player who goofs big-time.
- Set up a wager pool for inning and final game scores.
- Post numbered trivia questions on the walls (don't forget the bathroom). Guests write answers for each question on slips of paper for a prize drawing.
- Sing along to "The National Anthem" and "Take Me Out to the Ball Game."
- At the seventh inning, take a walk, or run the bases in your yard or parking lot.

Refreshments
- Standard ballpark fare: peanuts, Cracker Jacks, hot dogs, burgers, popcorn, pretzels, potato chips, ice-cream bars, Gatorade, soda, and beer (hawk the food to your guests from "around the neck" cardboard trays)
- Snacks served in baseball hats, mitts, and so on

Prizes/Favors
- Baseball key chains, magnets, pens, pencils, note pads, hats, T-shirts
- Customized baseball card for the guest of honor (See Resources, #16.)
- Trivia games

Part Four
PARTY TACTICS

This section outlines several popular tactics used in planning parties and celebrations, each with a definite set of rules or strategies that, when followed, will ensure the party's success. Along with the basic steps, each tactic plan also provides helpful tips and innovative twists to guide you.

Costume and Come As You Are parties give guests clothing suggestions, from extremely well-planned to impromtu attire. These party tactics either encourage guests to be themselves, or to go to elaborate efforts to be someone, or something, else.

Outdoor, Tailgating, Progressive, and Treasure/Scavenger Hunt party tactics are geared toward fresh air celebrations. Your guests, whether on the move or firmly planted in a lawn chair, will party together in the bright sunlight or the glowing moonlight.

Potluck and Tasting tactics feature food and drink. Organizing a well-balanced potluck meal and conducting an authentic tasting activity present two sets of challenges. The extra effort necessary to plan events that revolve around food and drink usually reap great rewards in guest appreciation.

Surprise! Hosts go to elaborate and devious efforts to get to the point in their plan when that word is shouted and the guest of honor is truly overwhelmed. Fund-Raising is another tactic that holds surprises. The guest turnout and the final financial gain will always be at their peak when you follow a solid plan. On the other hand, Ongoing parties have fewer surprises, since the group or club gathers regularly for the same mutually enjoyable activity.

The tactics mentioned in this section can be used by themselves, or in conjunction with any of the party themes found in this book. Mix and match tactics and themes, for business and personal occasions, to create your own unique combination and your certain success.

COME AS YOU ARE

This concept is rarely used in its pure form because it may cause inconvenience and embarrassment. But if you are intrigued by the idea, and if you dare to be different, go ahead and plan your party with this tactic. Know, however, that your guests may not be home when you call, or may strongly oppose your invitation.

Trends
- The timing of the party shouldn't be too inconvenient. It isn't considered very cute or clever to call your guests at an ungodly hour to ensure that you find them in a state of undress or disarray. If you do this, you will ensure a low turnout—even among your best friends or close family.
- Guests appreciate receiving some warning. If you extend the invitation at a reasonable hour, or if you allow adequate lead time, your turnout will be more successful.

Tips
- Spring "instant" invitations on your guests at 5:00 P.M.—the best time to ensure that you are not interrupting dinner hour and that all guests are fully dressed. Those persons who have already prepared dinner can store it away for the next day.
- Choose a weekend morning for your party, such as 10:00 A.M. Some guests will show up in sleepwear, but most will have already dressed casually for the day.
- Have a Come-As-You-Were party instead. Choose a time, and have guests come dressed as they would have been dressed at that time. You may get a better response with this version of the party.

Note: Some forewarned guests will be semihonest and make only slight improvements to their appearance, while others (especially women) will claim that they always lounge around the house in full makeup and presentable clothing.

Twists
- Choose the time for your party, and deliver your invitations in person during that time of day, a few days before the party date. Take an instant photo of each guest as you drop off the invitations. Prominently display these photos at the party, and award medals or trophies to guests who show up looking exactly as they do in their photo.
- Arrange to have yourself surprised with an invitation delivery, too, with an accompanying instant photo.
- Go from house to house and actually collect your guests. (Dragging them kicking and screaming is a better way to describe your chore.)

COSTUME

The phrase "Come dressed as..." brings out the best and worst in people. Some folks can pull together the components of a prize-winning costume from their closet—not even the attic or the basement. Others would rather take a beating than go through the hassle of dressing up "goofy." Hosts must accommodate both of these perfectly acceptable attitudes.

Trends
- In the past, party-goers have been ordered to wear everything from the back end of a horse to a full-sized evergreen tree, complete with trimmings. So, they did! The poor souls scrounged for, borrowed, bought, rented, or hand-crafted their costumes, and then struggled through an evening of sweating, itching, and being miserable. They did this, knowing that their fate would be much worse if they did any less, and nearly fatal if they did nothing; hosts and costumed guests are known to be vicious in their treatment of those who make no serious attempt to create costumes.
- Attention, hosts! Demanding that guests wear costumes is very inhospitable.

Tips
- Use the following phrases when writing invitations to your next costume party: "Costumes optional," "Your version of...," "Those in costume may win a prize," "Dress up a little or a lot," and "Apathy will not be scorned." All your guests will then look forward to your party—even those who suffer from "costumaphobia" (who, by the way, will make dandy judges for your costume contest).
- Include names and addresses of costume resources with the invitations. This thoughtful gesture may even inspire Mr. "Never Wears a Costume" to loosen up.

Twists
- Ask guests to wear garments of certain colors, such as all white or all black. That is actually a great way to use your guests as part of the decor.
- Have your guests wear white castoff clothing, so they can paint all over each other.
- Announce that basic black is a must for Over-the-Hill party mourners.
- Throw a semicostume party. No, the guests do not come topless or bottomless, they simply dress formally from the waist up, and casually from the belt down. This costume idea solves the big crowd/small space problem, which requires guests to sit on the floor, stairways, shelves, balconies, and chair arms. You'll be amazed at the combinations your guests will devise.
- Have each guest bring a shopping bag filled with costume props to be worn by other guests. Your guests' creativity (and cruelty) will surface with this theme.
- Request that guests wear entertaining costume accessories, such as crazy ties, wacky sunglasses, hats that best personify the wearer, or bizarre vests. This way, your guests can easily put together some sort of costume, and the theme accomplishes the goal of bringing everyone together in a common effort.

FUND-RAISING

All kinds of organizations hold fund-raisers: schools, churches, teams, organizations, charitable groups, and even businesses. Planning a profitable and successful fund-raiser is complicated by the facts that you have to rely on volunteer help and that competition for charitable contributions is fierce. A successful fund-raiser requires creativity, hard work, and business expertise.

Trends
- Gala dinner/dance evening parties top the list of fund-raising events. Guests enjoy a fine meal, entertainment, and, for added excitement, a silent, live auction.
- Family fund-raising events are also very popular, since they not only benefit a worthy cause, but provide an opportunity for parents to spend quality time with their children.
- Another trend is to combine charitable fund-raising with a fashion show, art exhibit, or restaurant/bar grand opening.

Tips
- Have modest goals for a first-time event. Selling 500 tickets at $10 each will be easier than selling 100 tickets at $50 each—and the end results are the same, anyway. Five hundred people will buy more auction items, and the exposure to your organization will be five times greater.
- Remember that ticket sales is the most important part of any fund-raising event. Be sure to have your ticket sales team in place and active before you spend a lot of time planning any other event details. If you don't sell any tickets, you will not have to plan anything, anyway.
- Decide on the party decor based on decorative items you can obtain inexpensively or for free: attics, garages, warehouses, and even storage rooms of local department stores may be virtual treasure troves of decorative material. Do your research, and you will save a lot of money.
- Call upon local amateur or semiretired talent for the entertainment at your event.
- Enlist the services (volunteer, of course) of a professional event planner to meet with your steering committee, either at the very beginning of the project, to help with the basic plan, or later, to troubleshoot. A professional will know about current trends, up-to-date resources, wholesale buying, and local suppliers who are most likely to donate or discount for your event.
- Don't think that table decor has to be identical; just be sure to follow a color scheme or a theme.
- Don't think that the more volunteers you have, the better. If you line up three times as many volunteers as you will need, one-third will drop out, one-third will forget what to do, and the core team will do all the work.

Note: When you prepare the room for an initial volunteer recruitment meeting, provide less chairs than the expected number of attendees. Then, when you add more chairs for the extra people, everyone will think that the turnout was much better than you expected and that enthusiasm is high for your project.

Twists

- A few days before the fund-raiser, have a gala event at which the guests decorate the tables as a party activity. Recruit the guests to sell seats for the table he or she decorated. Award prizes for the most creative tabletop design. This theme is popular for corporate executives or business owners who like to invite their special customers or clients to a gala event.
- Get a Standing Room Only turnout for a family event by sending invitations to the children, with instructions to bring the folks. You can rest assured that these invitations will be heeded.
- Be on the lookout for new businesses, especially restaurants, that might be interested in having a grand opening to benefit your organization. Your group produces the event; the restaurant shows off its food, drink, and service; and the guests pay admission that goes to the fund—everybody wins.
- Plan fund-raising events during the holiday season, and provide guests an opportunity to get some shopping done; auctions, sales, raffles, and sweepstakes drawings all accomplish that end.
- Invite local authors or artisans to sell their works at your holiday gala, and arrange to have them give part of the proceeds to your organization. Guests can shop, meet the authors/artists, and contribute to the fund.

ONGOING

Some get-togethers are so great that the group of guests is inspired to schedule regular gathering times. These groups meet four, six, or even twelve times a year to Party On!—ongoing, that is.

Trends
- Guests come together to accomplish a special goal related to a hobby, pastime, or interest. They combine the activity with refreshments and good company.
- In addition to scheduling get-togethers for the group members, the host sometimes plans "guest" events by inviting additional guests—as potential new members, or simply to enjoy the activity.

Tips
- Make sure that all members of the group share the interest around which the party is structured. For example, if you have a gourmet club in which group members take turns cooking for the group, all members should like to cook, not just eat.
- Schedule a time for the next meeting at the end of the previous one; this get-together may be the only time all group members are present at the same time.
- Keep records and mementos from all events to create a reference file available to all group members when planning future events.
- Document all activities with photos, videos, and comments. If you get a lot of fun stuff, create a media presentation that may turn into an annual event.

Twists
Create a club around any interest or activity. Following are some ideas:
- Board Game Club: Board-game enthusiasts gather to play, play, play.
- Book Club: Serious readers, or not-so-serious readers, discuss assigned books.
- Christmas Craft Club: Craft aficionados gather to make gifts for the holidays.
- Cooking Club: Budding chefs take turns preparing favorite recipes for the group.
- Dancing Club: Ballroom, Latin, contemporary, or any other kind of dance lovers gather at home or at a dance hall to learn and show off new moves.
- Investment Club: Money- and future-conscious people gather to report on, and then pool funds to make, investments.
- Party Planning Club: Party animals gather to help each other plan and produce upcoming parties. Club members create a party pool of equipment and supplies, and make group purchases to save money.
- Photo Album Club: Photography buffs, or those who want to have a nice photo album, gather to update their photo albums, using special preservation and decoration methods to enhance their photo memories.
- Quilting/Sewing Club: Guests meet to help each other finish large projects.
- Specific Collections Club: Collectors get together to share information, swap extras, or plan to produce or attend conventions.
- Travel Club: Travel enthusiasts gather to plan and to go on trips.

OUTDOOR

The wonderful outdoors is the ideal site for many celebrations and special events. The beauty of nature, the abundance of space, and the proximity to a lake or playground are some of the appeals. A gathering of family, friends, neighbors, or workmates in an outdoor setting has a built-in feeling of freedom and relaxation.

Trends
- Weddings, company picnics, fund-raising functions, reunions, and bazaars are all examples of events that are planned outdoors. Each type of party has its own set of concerns and arrangements, but one factor remains consistent from party to party: planning an outdoor event, especially in places where weather is temperamental, is the purest form of gambling.

Tips
- Include information on anticipated weather conditions and suggested attire with the invitations.
- Caution the ladies not to wear spike heels to an outdoor event: the heels may sink into, or cause their wearers to trip on, the grass.
- Provide clear, concise directions, and a map to direct guests to your event.
- Set out markers, such as signs, balloons, or flags, leading guests to event parking; then assign guidepersons to accompany guests to the exact event site.
- Always locate food stations, guest seating, and reception lines in the shade, under a tent or canopy, if necessary.
- Serve perishable foods on beds of crushed ice (or use "blue ice" packs), and leave such foods out for only short periods of time.
- Place a piece of plywood, one-foot square, under all table legs, to prevent tables from tipping or sinking into the ground.
- Provide excellent lighting on all walkways, using electric lamps or luminaria lights. (See Party How-To's, #9.)
- Be sure to spray the area for insects at least eight hours before the party, to prevent any uninvited pest guests.
- Provide enough toilet facilities for all the guests. For large parties, rent a Porta-Potty (two, if necessary) to set up at your outdoor site. Designate one for Ladies, and the other for Ladies and Gents. Equip each one with a mirror, a basket of moist towelettes, and a can of air freshener.
- Hire high-school or college students to supervise young children and to lead them in games and activities.
- Have ample sheltered seating for ill or elderly guests, in good or bad weather.
- Always have a backup plan in case the weather does not cooperate!

Twists
- Have your guests bring blankets and quilts for an old-fashioned picnic.
- Organize food-eating contests; outdoor events are ideal for such contests. Use plastic garbage bags as contestant covers: simply cut out holes for head and arms.

POTLUCK

The prospect of preparing huge quantities of food does not thrill all hosts. Many party planners love to decorate and entertain, but fall apart in the cooking department. Enter the Potluck party! A potluck party theme saves the host considerable time, stress, and expense, and best of all, it encourages the host to entertain more often.

Trends
- Careful coordination of menu items is essential to the success of the meal, especially for an intimate sit-down dinner. The host should discuss the menu with the guests to decide on the most reasonable and logical food assignments—someone who can't cook very well can be assigned to bring rolls or beverages.
- Potluck contributions to a larger party or picnic can be more spontaneous and creative, but they still need a little guidance.

Tips
- Prepare a menu, and assign items when guests call to RSVP.
- Do not simply suggest a category, such as salad, dessert, or snack: be specific. Many foods fall in those categories, and not all of them go well together.
- Do not ask a guest to prepare their favorite recipe, and leave it at that. This kind of freedom will frequently result in duplicated recipes.
- Avoid assigning categories according to each guest's last initial. (One hostess did so for a family party, and realized too late that 60 percent of the guests had the same last name—and also a flair for green Jell-O.)
- Choose foods that travel well and that do not require extensive or complicated preparation. All the food should require only a last-minute touch.
- Request that guests bring food in serving containers, so you won't have to transfer all those items to other dishes immediately before the party.
- Always request a response to your invitations, rather than asking people to respond only if they cannot attend. By asking your guests to respond in either case, you not only ensure an accurate head count for efficient planning, but you are then also able to establish whether everyone actually received the invitation. About a week before the event, call each person who hasn't responded to confirm their attendance.

Twists
- Have your guests take home leftovers of the food they prepared (you will usually have plenty of leftovers). Provide plastic take-home containers for this purpose, and let your guests take the party home with them!
- Create a neatly typed tent card for each dish, listing its name (real or made-up), ingredients, contributor, and any other interesting data. This decorative touch adds to the table's beauty, and makes traveling through the buffet line an entertaining and enlightening activity.

PROGRESSIVE

One of the easiest ways to entertain is to have the party at someone else's house! Actually, have it at a few other houses, in addition to your own.

Trends

- A progressive party moves from home to home, public place to public place, business to business, boat to boat, park to park, or any combination thereof. Most commonly, though, the progressive party plans a multicourse dinner, and arranges for each course to be served at a different place. The host at each location is responsible for the food, beverages, and decor.
- Neighborhood parties are the most convenient progressive parties, since guests can walk from spot to spot, enjoy cocktails or wine, and not worry about driving.
- The basic plan is as simple as assigning the four courses: appetizers and cocktails; soup, salad, and wine; entrée and wine; and dessert, coffee, and after-dinner drinks.

Tips

- Decide on a number of people each location can accommodate. Most homes can comfortably accommodate a maximum of sixteen people.
- Consider providing additional activities during each stop. Taking photos, awarding prizes, or enjoying any other entertainment would add zest to the party.
- Be careful about drinking and driving. If possible, travel from place to place as a group, with one designated driver.

Twists

Consider the following popular themes for progressive parties:

- International Party: Each stop of the party represents a different country, with corresponding food and beverages. Guests receive passport-like invitations, which are signed at each stop, and they also receive souvenir party favors, appropriate to the country represented.
- Bus Party: The host transports guests from place to place by bus, providing food and beverages during rest stops along the way. The stopping places don't have to be restaurants or bars; they can be parks or public places where you have made arrangements for refreshments and activities for your guests. A variation on this theme may include surprising the guest of honor with special guests at each stop.

Note: These themes take detailed planning, arranging, and coordinating, but the result is always a spectacular and memorable event.

SURPRISE

One of the most popular party tactics is the surprise party. Since the guest of honor is probably expecting something, the planner is challenged to pull off the surprise. The surprise element adds stress to the host's job of planning the party, but the result is almost always worth it.

Trends
- The strategies for planning a surprise party are quite simple, but crucial. Nothing is more frustrating or disappointing than making elaborate plans to surprise the guest of honor and having the biggest surprise be on you!
- A surprise party works best anywhere other than your home—at a close friend's or neighbor's home, a restaurant or recreational venue, or an outdoor site.
- A semisurprise party removes almost all anxiety: Tell the guest of honor that you are planning something, but leave almost all the details of the party as a complete surprise.

Tips
- Plan your party for a date before or after the actual celebration date (such as a birthday), to throw the guest of honor off track.
- If the party is planned at your home, have RSVP responses taken elsewhere, find a way to occupy the guest of honor while you do party-related tasks, provide another place to prepare food and decorations and to store other party supplies, and organize parking and/or transportation for guests.
- Arrange to have the guest of honor occupied with a friend or two on the day of the party. (Make sure that the friends know about the party and will deliver the guest of honor to the appointed place at the appointed time!)
- Emblazon the word SURPRISE on your invitation, and clearly explain all party strategies and suggestions: time of arrival, parking, gift policy, dress code, and schedule of events.
- Set up a voice-mail box to collect responses and to avoid inconvenient phone calls to your home or office. Reiterate all party details on the recorded greeting.
- Tell your guests to arrive one hour before the guest-of-honor's scheduled arrival. Leave a safety window of fifteen minutes before and after that time, to avoid awkward encounters in the doorway.
- Synchronize watches with the person delivering the guest of honor to the party.
- Instruct the guests how to behave before the party when they encounter the guest of honor, who will become suspicious if all close friends and relatives fail to acknowledge the event (usually a birthday or an anniversary).
- Encourage carpooling to avoid having large numbers of cars parked in front of the party location. For large parties, organize a shuttle service, so guests can park off site (for example, in the local market parking lot).
- Post a greeter/director at the entrance or gate of your party site. (Use cellular phones for covert communications.) Choose a person unknown to the guest of honor.

Twists

- Have guests arrive as a group to surprise the guest of honor at home. The surprise party starts when guests march in with food, decorations, music, and gifts. The following party themes work well with this tactic: Brunch Pajama Party, Sweets and Surprises, Dessert and Coffee, and Surprise Potluck Parade.

- Arrange a Step-by-Step Surprise Party: Have guests wait at different stops on a walking route, and arrange a party site within walking distance. Then, take the guest of honor for a walk, heading toward the party site, and passing all the "guest" stops. By the time you arrive at the party site, you will have collected all the guests.

- Always—I repeat, always—arrange to videotape all preparty activities and comments. The opportunity to enjoy this part of the party is a true gift for the guest of honor.

TAILGATING

For a casual, outdoor party, what can be better than entertaining from the back of a hatchback, station wagon, van, or truck? Minimum preparation, maximum fun.

Trends
- Although this method of entertaining is usually associated with attending a sports event, it can also be the main theme for a party.
- Any menu is fine, but if you want to follow tradition, serve grilled and barbecued meals, with all the proper accompaniments. A pig roast is a great parking-lot activity for tailgating. However, someone must "pig-sit" the roasting feast while guests are away enjoying events.
- Potluck is a popular tactic used to share the work and expense of the party. The host assigns particular items to all participating vehicles, which then serve as tailgate serving stations: ice and beverages; cold salads; rolls, breads, and buns; desserts; liquor; serving utensils and supplies.

Tips
- Have guests move from station to station, collecting their meals. This is especially good for guests who will soon be sitting for hours at a spectator event.
- Set up lawn chairs and use TV trays. You may also want to add portable tables for the tailgate overflow buffet.
- Provide lighting, if necessary. For evening events, hang strings of battery-operated lights to decorate and illuminate the tailgates.

Twists
- Plan activities, such as running a betting pool for games, tossing Frisbees, watching portable TVs, and dancing to live or recorded music, to keep the tailgaters entertained.
- Create a game of Pin the Tail on the Gate: Paint a target somewhere on the vehicle, and use team logos or circular photos of the guest of honor as the "tails."
- If the tailgating party is planned for a particular person, organize a progressive gift collection activity: Have the guest of honor walk from vehicle to vehicle to receive gifts. Stage a humorous gift ceremony at each stop. For a guest of honor who is a sports fan, arrange that each gift be a piece of apparel with a team logo. Have the guest of honor don each gift after opening it.
- Conduct a holiday Trim-the-Tailgate contest: Parade all the contestants on a drive through your neighborhood. Present awards, and crown royalty as part of your event.

TASTING

Treat your guests to a tasting event, featuring any "tastable" that strikes your fancy—from beer to burgers, or wine to wieners. If your guests are connoisseurs, seek an expert's advice on proper tasting protocol. However, if most of your guests don't know the difference between a vintage vino and a basement brew, your tasting event can follow your own rules and guidelines.

Trends
- An authentic wine-tasting event requires more preparation than an informal tasting event. You may want to solicit your local liquor store for advice on wine selection. If possible, arrange to have one of their representatives moderate the tasting.
- A tasting event is just that—tasting. The idea is not to eat or drink large quantities of anything. Rather, the idea is to fully appreciate and compare the qualities of a number of different foods or beverages. So, serve very small portions of anything being tasted.
- In an authentic tasting, the food or beverage is not always consumed, it is, instead, swished, gargled, or even spit out. However, unless you are entertaining real wine aficionados, your tasting event need not run that scrupulously true to form.

Tips
- Send a plastic fork, straw, or tiny sample cup along with, or attached to, the invitations.
- Provide an official rating sheet and pencil for each guest, at an authentic or spoof tasting event.
- Award blue ribbons for the best, sweetest, sourest, and so on, as applicable.
- Have each guest bring an item to enter into a tasting contest.
- Give prizes and favors that match your tasting theme. For example: ice-cream dippers, homemade jellies, wine openers, cookie jars, and exotic food items.

Twists
- Design a tasting event based on the guest-of-honor's passion: beer or wine, chili, baked potatoes, pasta, chocolate, ethnic foods, or fast foods.
- Have a spoof tasting event, with a sampling of such items as pickles, ice cream, French fries, or cookies. Such an event can be a lot of laughs when conducted in an ultraserious manner.

TREASURE/
SCAVENGER HUNT

Planning a "hunt" of this kind requires a lot of work and coordination. You will have to select from many types of hunts, depending upon your guests, your site, and your budget. Your efforts will be well spent, though, when you activate your guests' competitive spirits for a wonderfully wild and successful party.

Trends
- Many hunts combine the elements of clue-based hunts and regular scavenger hunts, for an independent, yet guided, event.
- The host provides a variety of refreshments during the event: light appetizers and beverages before the hunt, "traveling treats" and nonalcoholic beverages taken along for the hunt, and a bountiful buffet after the hunt.
- Some groups establish an annual hunting event and have an elegant, engraved trophy that changes hands every year, thus adding an extra competitive touch.

Tips
- Don't make the hunt too hard or too easy; it should be hard enough to be interesting, yet easy enough so as not to be discouraging.
- Ask someone who will not attend the party to read your clues to establish their workability.
- Always walk through your plan before the party, to test and time it.
- Plan any outdoor scavenger hunts for children to take place before dark.
- Be sure to have designated drivers for hunt events that require driving to gather items. Hire college students as designated drivers as a less-expensive alternative to a pricey limousine hunt.
- Take space restrictions into account when planning treasure hunts. For hunts in small areas, simply have the guests gather information to complete a form. For example, tie numbered tags on hunt items, and tell guests to quickly find and correctly list the tagged items.
- Award prizes to members of the winning teams.

Twists
- Take instant photos of guests taking part in zany activities.
- Conduct a mall treasure hunt for a unique event. Be sure to clear all arrangements with mall management and affected establishments. (See Resources, #57.)
- Play a sit-down, table-trivia treasure hunt: Divide guests into teams, and have them race to come up with trivia answers.
- Organize a do-it-before-you-come scavenger hunt: As part of the invitations, instruct guests to collect obscure item(s) and to bring those items to be admitted to the party. These items could include instant photos of guests in outrageous costumes, photos of guests with local celebrities, or photos of guests participating in very out-of-character activities.

Part Five
PARTY-PLANNING HELPERS

Throughout the book you have been referred to this section for ideas and tips on planning your special occasions. The information in this section is divided into four parts: Party Tips, Party How-To's, Resources, and the Theme-at-a-Glance Grid.

The Party Tips section provides general ideas and suggestions for every stage of party planning, such as Invitations, Guest Comfort, Music and Entertainment, and so on. Before you plan your next party, read through the Party Tips section for a heap of ideas to guide and inspire you in your planning.

In the Party How-To's section you will find brief instructions for creating certain objects mentioned in the book. These are special items I have discovered in my travels through partyland—things that can be produced for very little money and yet will create a significant impact on your party and your guests. Gather a group of crafters, and turn the creative session into a party by adding refreshments, music, and appreciation gifts for your helpers—all following your theme, of course. This session will not only provide you with an extra excuse to party, but it will give you an opportunity to have a trial party run before the actual event.

In the Resource section you will find a list of sources for party supplies, personalized items, unique products, and more. There's even a long list of party-related Web sites.

The grand finale of the book is the Theme-at-a-Glance Grid, accompanied by the Theme Selection Worksheet and the Planning Worksheet. These organizational tools will save you considerable time selecting themes applicable to your particular occasion.

PARTY TIPS

1. Party/Event Planning

- Theme-party brainstorning is accomplished by gathering a few of your most creative friends and/or family members to dream up all the possible themes and their accompanying details.

- Begin your planning by gathering the names of good vendors from your friends, family, and associates. Get contact names, prices, and inside tips for each supplier.

  As you contact vendors, make a file card for each one you think you might use, now or in the future. For each company, include a contact name, address, and phone number, along with items, style numbers, prices, and ordering data. As your planning progresses, jot down the date and content of any conversations you have with vendors. This card file will be a priceless diary and organizational tool for your current party and for many others to come. (For efficient party planning, use copies of the Planning Worksheet at the back of this book.)

- Save items from a loved one's wedding—invitations, programs, preserved flowers, decorations, gown fabric swatches, favors, napkins, cassettes of meaningful music—to be used for the first wedding anniversary celebration. Save the wedding items, as well as items from anniversary parties, to use for future anniversaries. In years to come, these items will bring precious memories.

2. Invitations

- Surprise your guests with clever invitations. The invitation sets the tone for the party and can even "start" the party by getting the recipients excited and enthusiastic about attending.

- If you are planning to use unusual packaging for the invitations or the envelopes, send a sample to yourself to see how it travels. The sample doesn't have to be the exact invitation or item that you have planned, just materials of comparable weight, design, and packaging.

- Do not put paper or metallic confetti in envelopes, even though it might seem like a festive idea. The confetti can be very inconvenient when it falls out into a person's coffee cup, computer/typewriter keyboard, or onto carpeting, where it will seem to multiply. If you want to be all-out festive, glue a few confetti pieces or other light items to the end of a ribbon that is attached to the inside of your invitation. When the envelope is opened, the confetti will drop, your party will begin, and the guest will be turned on—not off.

- Do not use "regrets only" on your invitation. This kind of response will only let you know who is not coming, and you will have no way of knowing whether all guests received their invitations. Request a "yes" or "no" response, then follow up with guests who did not respond, to make sure all invitations were received.

- Rent a voice-mail box to collect party reservations, especially when planning surprise parties or when calls would normally come to your office. An RSVP voice-mail greeting that matches your theme, recorded with music or sound effects in the background, will not only be more entertaining for the caller, but it will make your life less complicated. (See Resources, #25.)

- Add intrigue to your invitation by directing the guests to read an ad in the local newspaper, where they will find the RSVP phone number and/or password.

- List information on the Internet. Guests who do not have access to the Net will have to be resourceful in getting the data.

3. Guest Comfort

- Make guests feel welcome at large parties by having an official greeter direct arriving guests—from the coatroom, seating assignments, or name tags, to the reception line, bar, or punch bowl.

- For parties taking place in a hotel or condo, post a large sign, or better yet, a person at the entrance to direct guests to the party area. Place additional signs along the way, with funny sayings to amuse and lead guests.

Just for Fun
- Put signs, posters, props, or live/recorded theme music in the elevator to greet guests.

4. Name Tags

- Attach a name tag just below the right shoulder, so it is in direct line of one's eye when shaking another's hand.

- Lay out printed name tags in alphabetical order for arriving guests. Have extra tags on hand for rewrites or unexpected guests.

- Never allow guests to write their own name tags! Recruit someone to prepare the tags for arriving guests.

- Print names in large, bold, block letters—first name only, first name and last initial, or full name, whichever fits your group.

- Provide a handy, attractive container for discarding the self-adhesive tag backings.

Just for Fun
- Under each name, write a short description of each guest's relationship to the guest of honor (for example, "Bob's neighbor," "Bob's college pal," "Bob's Boss," and so on).

- Write a personal tidbit on each guest's name tag (for example, "Was Miss Iowa," "Collects bugs," "Passed bar exam," and so on).

5. Table Assignments and Seating Place Cards

- Always assign tables (not necessarily exact seats) for a dinner party. The assignment tells your guests that you have "reserved a place for them" and takes away their anxiety about trying to find a place to sit.

- Limit seat-by-seat assignment to small dinner parties.

- Write table assignments on name tags for easy seating directions.

- Write names and assigned table numbers on tags attached to party favors. Arrange the tags, with the favors, alphabetically on a table.

- For casual events, use food for table assignments. For example, write table numbers on shiny apples, tiny baskets of candy, or individual bags of popcorn, and hand those out instead of cards. Or, create table markers and decor to match the food items, and have the guests match their food item to the table marker (for example, all apples sit at the table with the basket of apples in the middle, and so on). The second version works best at parties with fewer than six tables.

- Seat couples together or apart, whichever you think best. Assigning seats randomly is an adventure, because it mixes and matches people who might never meet if left to their own devices.

- Place large numbers on each table so they can be easily discovered. Numbers written on helium-filled Mylar balloons are decorative and easy to spot. Attach each numbered balloon to a centerpiece.

- Schedule rotation seating at dinner parties with a maximum of sixty-four guests; this involves guests changing tables after each course. Rotation seating is a delightful and innovative concept, especially appropriate for reunions.

- If you decide to have an adults-only party, be clear about it on your invitation by using a term such as "Mom and Dad's Night Out." However, if children are usually a part of your family occasions—such as weddings, anniversaries, retirements, reunions, holidays, or birthdays—they will have to be invited. Unfortunately, not all parents teach their children proper "company" behavior or keep their children in tow at social gatherings. Set up special activities and entertainment for children, and if you feel it necessary, hire a young adult to oversee the group. Children and parents will appreciate this special attention.

- Tell wedding ushers to suggest "back-of-the-church baby row" seating for guests with small children, so that they can slip out gracefully if the child starts to cause a commotion. Ushers' speech: "We've saved this special row for those of you with young children, so that you can duck out easily if the child gets restless during the ceremony." Better yet, suggest to the guests to make use of the church nursery.

6. Decor

- Be sure to use floating candles properly—the water level shouldn't be higher than half the container. Flames too close to the rim will heat and crack the glass.

- Save money by creating table centerpieces using party favors. For example, a decorative basket filled with gaily wrapped packages makes a beautiful centerpiece when placed on a low pedestal (inverted cottage cheese container covered with a velvet or Mylar drape) and trimmed with elegant ribbons, streamers, and, for extra festivity, helium balloons.

- Do not feel that all the centerpieces have to be identical. Spray-paint a variety of baskets the same color, and fill them with the same flowers and greens. The effect will be marvelous.

- Use cookbooks as tasteful and decorative additions to your buffet table. Stand the cookbooks up, with the covers in clear view, and arrange fruit, vegetables, bread, wine, or fancy cooking utensils around them. Add colorful linens, flowers, plants, and/or interesting serving pieces.

- Use collections, such as books, antique cups and saucers, paper weights, bells, candlesticks, or tin boxes, in table decor. To display them, set them on inverted boxes, bowls, or baskets, either draped with cloth or left plain.

- Place votive candles in small juice, wine, and champagne glasses, snifters, or any decorative glass containers. Search thrift stores or garage sales for these containers. Place two or three (matching or not) on each table to create a romantic or glamorous effect. Battery-operated candles are another option for table decor in rooms where lit candles are not allowed.

- If inviting kids, provide them with paper tablecloths upon which each child's place setting has been drawn, ready to be filled in with colored markers. The design should include the child's name, an arrow pointing to his or her place, a plate, utensils, and a beverage container. Supply markers for the children to color the designs.

- Place mirrored tiles under centerpieces, on buffet tables, or around candles to add to the elegance of a table setting. These shiny, shimmery squares are available at discount stores for about $1 each, which is a real bargain, because they can be used over and over again.

- Use round mirrors instead of, or in addition to, mirrored tiles. These mirrors are available at florists' supply houses. Mirrors are more expensive than tiles, but they are more decorative, and can also be used frequently.

- Have a supply of twinkle lights on hand. These party staples can be draped on trees, stairways, and banister rails, around windows and mirrors, and over mantles. Battery-operated twinkle lights can be used in centerpieces or other decorative arrangements for a fantastic look.

- Add backdrops, props, and custom-made decorations to any party. Contact your local high-school/college art departments or school of art to find students who will paint backdrops or make props and custom-made decorations. In some cases, the students can get credit for the project and you'll have to pay only for materials—it works out for everyone. After your party, give the items to the students, a theater group, or a party rental company (with the agreement that you can use them again).

- Think of ways to reduce the costs of renting decorations and various equipment. If planning an event in a banquet space, explore the possibility of sharing decorations or rental equipment with the host of an event that will take place the day before or after yours. Such sharing can help save on delivery/pick-up charges, and many rental places have multiple-day rates. This is a great way to have more and pay less.

7. Activities

- Host a mystery party by using a Mystery game designed for eight. The game details must be duplicated, rotations organized, and clues prepared—a lot of work, but worth it. For a successful mystery party, follow these steps:
  1) Get a body-and-soul commitment from guests, by phone, in multiples of eight. Then send out the official invitations.
  2) Assign a character role to each guest. For instance, if you have invited forty people, you will have five of each character. If you like, tell the guests to dress in costumes appropriate to their characters.
  3) Run the party as a progressive game by moving guests to a different table after each course. (The guests will pick up their beverages and utensils with each move.)
  4) Play the game exactly as it would be played for eight people, guests always staying in their characters. Award prizes for best costume and for solving the mystery. (See Resources, #4, for more information about mystery parties.)

- Make a video of the guests' participation and antics, especially if taking guests to an activity site, then back home. Watch the videos during dessert.

- Play name-tag games as party mixers. Such games are a good way to get your guests to mingle, and they are easy to devise. Some that work well are trivia games (in which the guests have to match the questions to the answers), scrambled-word games (in which guests match the scrambled words to the unscrambled versions), and coded-tag games (in which tags are coded with colors, numbers, or objects, and guests have to find the matching color, number, or object). Be sure to neatly write (with a different colored ink than the name) the question, word, or number on each name tag. Guests who make matches win prizes for speediness and receive blank slips to enter in a prize drawing.

- Devise a similar game by listing theme-related questions on a 8½-by-11-inch sheet of paper, leaving blanks to be filled in with answers found on guests' name tags. Mount copies of the questionnaire (one per guest) on poster board, and attach a pencil on a string.

- Use instant photos of guests to create a game that encourages guests to interact.
  1) Attach a safety pin, paper clip, or other small item that matches your theme to each name tag before handing them out to the guests.
  2) Take instant photos of each guest or couple.
  3) Write a number under each photo, and display all photos in a prominent place. The number serves as an ID number for each guest.
  4) Have the guests look up the numbers, and tell them that they have to greet others using the number, instead of the person's name. Guests must relinquish the item attached to their name tags to anyone who greets them with their ID number.
  5) Award a prize to the guest who accumulates the most items. (The guest can stick the accumulated items to his or her name tag, collar, or anywhere.)
  6) Give photos to guests as party favors.

- Play a trivia mixer game:
  1) Display trivia or theme questions and/or photos around the event site.
  2) Provide a quiz form to each guest.
  3) Have the guests complete their forms by answering the questions and identifying the photos.
  4) Award a prize to the guest who first completes the quiz form correctly (or who has the most correct answers).

8. Music and Entertainment

- Greet your guests with music or sound effects appropriate to your theme. Preferably, blast it out into the yard. But if that is not "neighborly," have the music playing out the front door. Circus themes call for calliope; patriotic themes require Sousa marches; and so forth.

- Add live or recorded music to any of the themes, for dancing and listening.

- Schedule a specific time for toasts, speeches, or presentations, then stay precisely on schedule. Alert guests of the time constraints so they will be prepared.

- Solicit audio- or videotaped messages for the guest of honor from guests who will not be able to attend. These messages will be the life of the party if presented all at once or interspersed throughout the event.

- Treat a This Is Your Life party as a major production, with staging, lighting, props, and audio engineering. Contact your college drama department, and recruit an aspiring theater major to produce the show.

9. Refreshments

- Label foods and drinks that are unusual or have gimmick, theme-related names. Place small, clearly printed tent cards in front of the items. For example, a label that says, "Take a look into your Tofuture!" in front of a plate of tofu, or "Let's Do the Twist" in front of a basket of pretzels at a Fifties party.

- Always give banquet-dinner guests a choice of entrées to accommodate today's varied preferences. Beef is less popular than it once was. Chicken is the safest. Some young couples feel that the wedding dinner should consist of their own personal favorite foods, thereby subjecting their guests to exotic or restricted menus. Guests must be considered, so be sure to serve meals that your guests will thoroughly enjoy.

- Plan alcoholic selection and service appropriate to your party. For large parties or weddings, anything goes. Hosts are opting for everything from totally non-alcoholic service to lavish open bars and complete dinner wine service. For events planned at a hotel or restaurant, budget restraints are the biggest deciding factor. Home-party hosts can be more generous with alcohol.

  Practices and personal beliefs regarding this important part of any party or event vary widely. For example: If you hold a large party at a public place, a nice balance of alcoholic beverages includes champagne or champagne punch during the reception, wine with the meal, and all other alcoholic beverages on a cash-bar basis. At more-casual parties, you might roll out the barrel of complimentary beer.

10. Prizes/Favors

- Instant photos are a must for almost every party. Having guests pose for the photos is a perfect party activity, and the photos are great favors. Create a photo setting with theme props, and position a sign or banner announcing the event (Bob's 50th Birthday Bash) behind the subjects so it appears in the photos.

- "Magazine-cover," Victorian-style, "guest's-head-on-funny-body," and "standing-next-to-celebrity" photos are very popular. With the addition of an inexpensive frame, these photos make ideal party favors. Cardboard folder frames can be decorated and personalized with the name of the event for low-cost and high-impact souvenir favors.

- Hats, T-shirts, mugs, bags, and dozens of other customized items make great party favors and provide another activity that will liven up your party.

- Party favors are fun to give and receive, but in many cases the items are of little or no use, and represent a huge waste of money. Party favors can be decorative, amusing, *and* useful. Following are some suggestions for fun and practical favors: refrigerator magnets, picture frames, note pads and pens, bud vases, trinket boxes, holiday ornaments, miniature photo albums, playing cards, mugs, sachets, paper weights, address/phone books, horoscope or "day you were born" certificates. All of these items can be personalized.

PARTY HOW-TO'S

Invitations

1. Crystal Ball Invitations

Supplies (for 1 invitation)
Envelope, to fit your invitation
Clear cellophane
A pair of scissors
Glue
Pen

Directions
1. Cut an approximately 3-inch circle on the invitation envelope, in the area where you would normally write the guest's address.
2. From the inside, glue a piece of cellophane over the opening.
3. Either on the invitation or on a separate piece of paper, draw a circle slightly smaller than the cut-out circle, so the line is visible through the opening.
4. In the drawn circle, write "There's a Party in Your Future." Write the name and address under the phrase.

Note: If you draw the circle on the invitation, make sure that all the writing shows through the window once you place the invitation into the envelope.

2. Invitation in a Beer Can

Supplies (for 1 invitation)
1 empty, dry beer can with an interesting label (open the pop-top a little, pour out the beer, and glue the top down with hot glue)
Metal shears or heavy-duty scissors
Ribbon
Small, lightweight, party-related items
1 self-adhesive, blank mailing/name-tag label
1 postage stamp, preferably self-adhesive

Directions
1. Cut a flap in the side of the bottle—about two inches high and three inches wide—with shears or scissors.
2. Roll up the invitation and tie it with a ribbon.
3. Insert the invitation and party-related items into the bottle through the flap.
4. Address the blank mailing label and place it over the flap.
5. Affix a postage stamp onto the label (it will not stick on the can). If using regular stamps, glue them on to be sure they will stick.
6. Mail a sample to yourself to make sure it travels well. If it does, repeat steps 1 through 5 to make enough for all the guests.

3. Invitation in a Cloth Bag

Supplies (for 1 invitation)
1 small bag of muslin, burlap, cotton, or faux suede (you can buy them or make
    them yourself with no-sew tape or glue)
2 pieces of twine or raffia
1 hunk of hay
1 small, lightweight item (toy tin star, cello-wrapped pretzel, or beef jerky)
1 self-adhesive, blank mailing/name-tag label
Markers
1 postage stamp, preferably self-adhesive

Directions
1. Fold the invitation, tie it together with twine, and tuck a hunk of hay in the knot.
2. Put the invitation into the bag, together with a party-related item.
3. Tie the bag closed with raffia or twine.
4. Draw a rope or country-design border on a blank mailing label. Print the return
    address and guest address on the label and attach it to the bag (you might have
    to glue the label onto some fabrics).
5. Affix a postage stamp onto the label (it will not stick on the bag). If using regular
    stamps, glue them on to be sure they will stick.
6. Mail a sample to yourself to make sure it travels well. If it does, repeat steps 1
    through 5 to make enough for all the guests.

4. Invitation in a Plastic Bottle

Supplies (for 1 invitation)
1 clean, dry, plastic beverage bottle with the cap securely screwed on
Ribbon
Small, lightweight, party-related items (silk flowers, candies, or tiny plastic toys)
1 self-adhesive mailing/name-tag label
1 postage stamp, preferably self-adhesive
Decorative stickers, paint, or magazine cutouts and glue

Directions
1. Cut a flap in the side of the bottle—about two inches high and three inches
    wide.
2. Roll up the invitation and tie it with a ribbon.
3. Insert the invitation into the bottle through the flap, and enclose small, light-
    weight, party-related items.
4. Decorate the blank mailing label to coordinate with your theme or color scheme,
    leaving room for the return address, guest address, and stamp. Attach the label
    to the bottle, completely covering the flap.
5. Affix a postage stamp onto the label (it will not stick on bottle). If using regular
    stamps, glue them on to be sure they will stick.
6. Decorate the bottle and cap with stickers, paint, or cutouts.
7. Mail a sample to yourself to make sure it travels well. If it does, repeat steps 1
    through 6 to make enough for all the guests.

5. Magical Invitations

Supplies

4-inch squares of variously colored tissue or nonraveling fabric, enough for all
   guests (decide on a "special" color, and make only 3 squares of that color)
Glue pen
Fine glitter
Sharp knife

Directions

1. Print the word "Poof" on the center of each square using a glue pen.
2. Sprinkle fine glitter on top of the glue. Shake off excess.
3. Use a sharp knife to cut a small slit about 1½ inches long—in a straight or curved
   line—in the middle of each invitation.
4. Pick up a tissue square in the middle of the nonglitter side, and tuck it into the
   invitation slot, so only a little color is visible.
5. Within the text of the invitations, instruct the guests to bring their square to the
   party for a prize contest.
6. Seal the invitation envelopes, and shuffle them before addressing them, so you
   don't know who will receive the invitations with the specially colored squares.
7. Conduct a prize drawing, with the color of the squares determining the prize.
   For example: Pink squares win customized (with guest-of-honor's name) pink
   magic markers; blue squares win blues audiotapes; and so on. Have special
   prizes for the holders of the specially colored squares.

Decor

6. Fish-Holding-Person Photo Front

(This is an all-purpose item for a Hunting/Fishing party; it serves as a decoration, a
fun activity, and a party favor.)

Supplies

Large sheet of cardboard (at least 6-foot high)
Paint
Pair of scissors

Directions

1. Paint a large (almost 6-foot) fish that is
   standing on its tail and holding a person in
   its fin by the person's feet.
2. Cut out a circle where the person's face
   would be.
3. Paint a banner above the fish to read one of
   the following:
   "The Big One That Didn't Get Away!" or
   "[Guest-of-honor's name] Catch of the
   Day"

4. Build a stand to prop up the poster upside down, so the person's head is on top. The guests can take turns placing their faces into the opening, while someone else photographs them. The photos, right-side-up, will resemble typical "fish-story" souvenirs and make great party favors.

7. Giant Postcard Posters

(These make dandy decorations for bon voyage, going away, or moving parties.)

Supplies (for 1 postcard)
Standard poster board, any color
Pen
Glue

Directions
1. Divide the card into two postcard sections—address/stamp and message—with a vertical line down the middle, like in a regular postcard.
2. Write a message that may have been written by the guest of honor.
3. Address it to a specific person, or to all guests as a group.
4. Draw a stamp and postmark, to indicate the place of origin.
5. Glue a travel poster, draw a picture, or create a collage on the picture side of the postcard (optional).
6. Hang the postcard from the ceiling mobile-style (if decorated on both sides), or display on a wall (if decorated on one side).

8. Hay Bale Boxes

Supplies (for 1 bale)
1 cardboard box
Hay (amount will vary depending on the size of the box)
Baling wire or rope (amount will vary depending on the size of the box)
Rocks, bricks, magazines, or other heavy objects

Directions
1. Fill box with rocks, bricks, magazines, or other heavy objects, to weigh it down.
2. Glue hay to the outer sides of cardboard cartons to make "bales."
3. Tie the bales with baling wire or rope.

9. Luminaria (lights in bags)

Supplies (for 1 candle)
1 white, plain brown, colored, or fancy-patterned lunch-sized paper bag
Fancy paper cutters
Metallic or plain acrylic paint
Paintbrushes
2 to 3 cups of sand
1 votive candle

172

Directions
1. Fold down the top of the bag twice to make a cuff.
2. Stencil or draw shapes all around the bag—stars, half moons, boots, flowers, and other party-theme-related designs.
3. Cut out the drawn shapes, or use fancy shape punchers (available in craft stores) to cut designs in the bag, and to make a border all around the top.
4. Outline the edges of the cutout shapes with glitter or paint. Draw additional designs, if you like.
5. Line the bottom of the bag with sand, and use the sand to secure a votive candle.
6. Use the glowing bags to line walkways, stairways, poolsides, driveways, or tops of patio walls.

10. Tissue-Paper Flowers

(These flowers are festive decoration staples to use in room and table decor, gift wrapping, and party favors.)

Supplies
2 20-by-30-inch sheets of tissue paper (size will vary according to planned use)
Pair of scissors
24-inch length of florist's wire or 1 paper-covered stem (available at craft stores)
Green florist's tape

Directions
1. Layer tissue-paper sheets with edges aligned. Fold the layered sheets in half lengthwise.
2. Cut along the fold line. You now have 4 10-by-30-inch pieces.
3. Layer all 4 pieces with edges aligned. Beginning at the shorter end, make 1-inch-wide fan folds along entire length of layered pieces, keeping folds and edges even. *Tip: Hold pieces in alignment with a staple at the center of each 10-inch end.*
4. Bend florist's wire in half, and slip wire over center of folded tissue paper; twist wire tightly. (See Diagram 1.) Use longer wire for longer stems. Cover the stems with florist's tape or ribbon. For a glitzy look, dip the wire in glue and then in glitter.
5. Cut the ends of the folded tissue paper to make rounded or pointed petals. (See Diagram 2.) Trim with novelty edge scissors for a nice effect.
6. To separate and fluff flower petals, begin at the center of the lower layer and pull up 1 layer of tissue paper at a time toward the center of the flower.

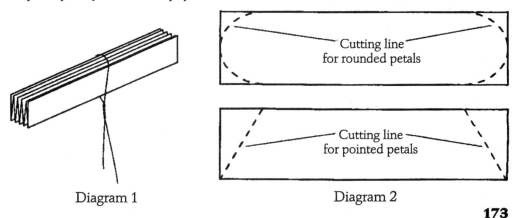

Cutting line
for rounded petals

Cutting line
for pointed petals

Diagram 1   Diagram 2

Variations
- Make smaller flowers by using 3 6-by-20-inch) pieces of tissue paper. (For larger flowers, expand the fold size, and use only 3 pieces of paper. You can experiment with these sizes.)
- Make multicolored flowers by using 2, 3, or 4 colors of tissue paper. For example, use 3 pieces of hot pink and 1 of yellow.
- Use printed, metallic, or iridescent tissue papers: they work wonderfully.
- Mix in 1 or 2 layers of tulle, especially for weddings.
- Use black, white, and silver paper to make a dramatic statement.
- Make gold-and-white flowers for anniversaries.
- Put a few spots of glue on each flower, then sprinkle with glitter for a festive touch.
- Use colored pipe cleaners for the stems, then wrap around napkin for a gala table decoration.
- Use the flowers as bows on gifts.
- Instead of making a stem, tie the flowers with ribbons to be worn in the hair or as a corsage (these make great favors).
- Use other materials: cellophane, Mylar, plastic.

Refreshments

11. Scarlett O'Hara Cocktail

Ingredients
1 part cranberry juice
2 parts lime juice
8 parts bourbon
Crushed ice

Directions
1. Combine all ingredients and shake.
2. Strain to remove the ice, and serve in martini glass.

Note: When 1 part=1 ounce, the above batch would make 3 cocktails.

Activities

12. Customized Bingo Cards
(This game is ideal for any party or gathering, especially for parties with casino or gambling themes.)

Supplies
An inexpensive bingo game, with more than enough cards for all players
Cardboard chips, for space covers

Directions
1. Design a bingo-card-style heading using the name of the guest of honor or the title of your event. If the name or title is 5 letters, your task is simple. However, most likely you will have to divide the letters to create a 5-letter header. For

For other themes appropriate for your occasion, see the theme grid on page 188.

example: AN-T-H-O-NY or J-E-SS-I-C-A, for first names; J-OH-N-SO-N, for last names; 50th-ANN-I-VER-SARY or GO-MU-SK-RA-TS, for events. (See Drawing 1.)

AN	T	H	O	NY
1	14	24	36	45
4	18	27	38	46
3	20		39	50
9	21	29	41	52
11	22	33	43	54

Drawing 1

2. Size your header to match the bingo cards, and paste the header onto a card.
3. Make copies of the card on sturdy paper or card stock, enough so that each guest can have 2 or 3 cards.
4. Write all the created numbers on card stock, and cut apart. For example: B1 becomes AN1, I12 becomes T12, and so on. (See Drawing 2.) Put all the cut-out numbers into a container.
5. Appoint a reader, who will pull the numbers out of the container and call them out loud. Have guests cover the corresponding spaces with cardboard chips, as in regular bingo, until someone calls out, "Anthony!" (which means that the person has covered all spaces in a straight line—up, down, or across).
6. After each game is finished, guests can clear their card, keep it for the next game, trade with another guest, or get another card.

AN	T	H	O	NY
1	12	23	34	45
AN	T	H	O	NY
2	13	24	35	46
AN	T	H	O	NY
3	14	25	36	47
AN	T	H	O	NY
4	15	26	37	48
AN	T	H	O	NY
5	16	27	38	49
AN	T	H	O	NY
6	17	28	39	50
AN	T	H	O	NY
7	18	29	40	51
AN	T	H	O	NY
8	19	30	41	52
AN	T	H	O	NY
9	20	31	42	53
AN	T	H	O	NY
10	21	32	43	54
AN	T	H	O	NY
11	22	33	44	55

Drawing 2

Note: Attach a photo of the guest(s) of honor to the backs of the bingo cards, and in the center "free" spot, to customize the cards (which will then make excellent party favors).

13. Dictionary Game

(This word game is fun for a group of 8 to 10 people. The object of the game is to stump other players with the meanings of obscure words.)

Supplies
Dictionary
Pencils, 1 for each player
Small, same-sized strips of paper (each player gets the same number of strips as there are players)
Score sheet, 1 for each player

Directions
1. Choose a player who starts the game. That person will be the Reader.
2. Have the Reader search the dictionary for a word that is completely unknown to all players (no cheating!).
3. All players write a made-up definition on a slip of paper. The Reader writes the correct definition. Everybody puts the slips into a container.
4. The Reader reads all definitions aloud, including the correct one, trying to make them all sound genuine.
5. Players guess the correct definition and write the definition on the score sheet.
6. Players pass their score sheet to another player for grading.
7. The Reader reads the correct definition. Players record the scores on the score sheets.
8. Choose another Reader, and start over.

For other themes appropriate for your occasion, see the theme grid on page 188.

Scoring
- Every player who guesses the correct definition gets 10 points.
- Every player whose definition is chosen by others gets 10 points for every person who chose the definition.
- The Reader gets 10 points for each wrong guess, and a bonus of 30 points if no one guesses the correct definition.

14. Fan Flirting

(As a party activity you can teach your guests one of the primary methods of romantic communication in the Victorian Era, taken from the *Young Ladies' Journal,* 1872.)

The code is as follows:
Fan fast—I am independent
Fan slow—I am engaged
Fan with right hand in front of face—Come on
Fan with left hand in front of face—Leave me
Fan open and shut—Kiss me
Fan open wide—Love
Fan half open—Friendship
Fan shut—Hate
Fan swinging—Can I see you home?

Prizes/Favors

15. "Clippin' Along" Minicar Favor

(This is an ideal party favor for your racy guests, and makes a great desktop souvenir for home or office.)

Supplies (for 1 favor)
1 juice glass or votive candle holder with a checkered trim (See Resources, #38.)
1 miniature car
Hot glue
Paper clips
Cellophane
Satin ribbon
Piece of paper and pen

Directions
1. Use hot glue to attach the bottom of a juice glass onto the top of a miniature car. (Be sure to center the glass exactly or the car will tip over.)
2. Place the car in the center of an 8-inch square of clear cellophane, and fill the glass with paper clips.
3. Pull cellophane up and around the car and glass, bunching the cellophane at the top.
4. Tie the bunched-up cellophane with a satin ribbon, making sure the paper clips won't fall out. Do not make a bow yet.
5. Write "Clippin' Along with (fill in the name of the guest of honor, company, or association)" on a small tag, punch out a hole, and attach the tag to the ribbon. Tie a bow.

16. Party Cracker Favor

Supplies

Cardboard tubes from toilet-paper, paper towels, or gift wrap—as many as you
    want, cut the same length
Miscellaneous small gift items:
    For Children: candy, toys, games, stickers, erasers, bandannas, jewelry, and so on
    For Grownups: handkerchiefs, silk scarves, perfume, lotion and other beauty
    products, spices, potpourri, candy, nuts, and so on
Wrapping paper, appropriate to the party theme: newspaper or magazine pages for
    Earth Day, birthday paper for birthdays, holiday paper for specific holidays, and
    so on)
Ribbons, tinsel, or star garlands
Markers or metallic pens

Directions

1. Tuck the appropriate gift items into the cardboard tubes.
2. Wrap with wrapping paper, leaving about 3 inches on each end.
3. Twist the extra paper, and tie with ribbons, tinsel, or star garlands.
4. Write each guest's name on a cracker with a marker or a metallic pen.

Miscellaneous

17. Greeting Card Postcard

Supplies (for 1 card)
1 used greeting card
Pair of scissors
Pen
1 postage stamp

Directions

1. Cut the front (the decorated half of the card, with a blank back) off the used
    greeting card.
2. Draw a line on the blank side, to separate the message area from the address
    area, as on a regular postcard.
3. Write the message and the address; attach a postcard stamp; and mail.

Note: Be sure that the postcard size is within legal postcard dimensions. If your
postcard is larger than the standard size, it will require a first class stamp.

RESOURCES

The list below includes the information you need to request more information. A half-page fax request sheet will cost less than a postcard, and it will also provide you with a record of your request. If the manufacturer sells only to the trade, they will give you the name of the retailer nearest you.

Theme Party Supplies

1. Advanced Graphics: Life-sized, cardboard, standup figures of celebrities. They also do custom orders of anyone you like.
Phone: (510) 432-2262 Fax: (510) 432-9259

2. Benson's Import Corp.: Props for island themes—palm trees, huts, bamboo curtains, shells, tiki lamps.
Phone: (714) 893-3217

3. Gamblers General Store: Hundreds of items for casino-style events.
Phone: (800) 322-2447 Fax: (702) 366-0329

4. Host Your Own Murder Mystery Party Game: Games designed for six to eight guests, which can be adapted and customized for larger groups, as described in this book. *The Lighter Side Catalog.*
Phone: (941) 747-2356

5. Kentucky Derby Party Kits & Equestrian Gifts (Trade Only): All kinds of ideas for a Kentucky Derby Party.
Phone: (800) 993-3279

6. The Lighter Side: Lighthearted Gifts & Delightful Surprises: Gimmicks, gadgets, and goofiness of all kinds for theme-party fun.
Phone: (941) 747-5566

7. M&N International, Inc. Catalog: The one-stop for ethnic theme-party supplies—items representative of dozens of countries are available. Phone: (708) 680-4700 Fax: (708) 816-1200

8. The Music Stand: Every imaginable item customized with musical motif, for ideal gifts, prizes, favors, or awards at music-theme parties
Phone (800) 414-4010

9. Paradise Products, Inc.: A catalog of "Fling Decorating Kits" for most themes in this book. Kits include decorations, favors, servingware, and costume props.
Phone: (510) 524-8300 Fax: (510) 524-8165
Address: P.O. Box 568, El Cerrito, CA 94530

10. Rick's Movie Graphics: Hundreds of posters and publicity photos from the movie and recording industries—perfect for vintage or contemporary party themes. Phone: (800) 252-0425

11. susan a designs: Imprintable theme-designed stationery (trade only). A large collection of imaginative designs for invitations, announcements, menus, and programs for every special event. Find them near you. Phone (508) 458-6700

Theme-Related Associations and Events

12. American Redneck Day (for a Labor Day Party)
Phone: (410) 758-0777
Address: American Redneck Trading Post Catalog; Ed Mason, National Director; 317 Fogwell Road, Centreville, MD 21617

13. Chase's Annual Events (for Tea Parties and many other parties): This is a big book, available at all libraries, that lists all the special commemorations, festivals, celebrations, "official" months, weeks, and days in calendar form. A good source of posters and printed materials. Simply write to the contact listed and request additional information or material.

14. Great American Beer Festival (for a Beer Tasting Party): The festival takes place September 26-28. Call shortly before the first of September to obtain posters or promotional materials.
Phone: (303) 447-0816
Address: Association of Brewers, P.O. Box 287, Boulder, CO 80306

15. National Stamp Collecting Month (For a Stamp Collecting Party): November is the official stamp collecting month.
Address: U.S. Postal Service, P.O. Box 557, Boalsburg, PA 16827-0557

Personalized and Customized Products

16. Big League Cards, Custom Sports Cards: Personalized cards for all sports and other specialty areas, such as music, books, or hobbies—for an ideal invitation enclosure, gift, favor, or prize.
Phone: (201) 692-8228
Address: 265 Cedar Lane, Teaneck, NJ 07666

17. Candy Bar Birth Announcements, Carson Enterprises: A full-sized chocolate bar wrapped with personalized, laser-printed information about the new baby. A most unique and "sweet" way to announce the news.
Phone: (513) 887-2211 Fax: (513) 785-2060

18. C.D. Designs: Hand-Painted Wine Labels: Full-color, original artworks to enhance wine bottles—to be used as decor, gifts, or prizes.
Phone: (413) 585-3580
Address: 78 Harrison Avenue, Northampton, MA 01060

19. International Star Registry: A way to name a star after the guest of honor. This gift costs approximately $35 and is ideal for any theme, especially one related to space, astrology, stars, or the future. It includes a certificate with the location of the ultra-personal celestial body.
Phone: (800) 282-3333

20. Laser-Imprintable Cardboard Visors: A way to totally customize decorative visors by using your laser printer. These are quite affordable for small or large groups. In Paper Direct Catalog.
Phone: (800) A-Papers Fax: (800) 443-2973

21. NewsFavors: Customized Crossword Puzzles: Pertinent information about your special event, including names, dates, and personal details, is woven into a crossword puzzle that may be used as an invitation, event activity, or souvenir favor, for both personal and business events.
Phone: (201) 670-0582
Address: P.O. Box 1144, Glen Rock, NJ 07452

22. Newsmakers by Dave Kohls: Personalized news articles engraved on metal and mounted on wood plaques. Ideal awards or gifts for personal occasions or business events.
Phone: (800) 579-7758 Fax: (805) 687-4762

23. Outrageous Fortunes: Custom Fortune Cookies: Your own message tucked inside a fortune cookie.
Phone: (612) 724-6115 (ask for Sunny Kwan)
Address: 326 Cedar Avenue, Minneapolis, MN 55454 (attn: Sunny Kwan)

24. Past & Future Favors: Personalized horoscope sheets or "what happened the day you were born" certificates for gifts, favors, or unique table icebreakers.
Address: Favors, 73-729 Manzanita Court, Palm Desert, CA 92260

25. SongSendsations: Custom Songs: Everything about an individual, couple, or group woven into a sing-along presentation. They also create RSVP voice-mail greetings for theme parties.
Address: Songs, P.O. Box 2200, Palm Desert, CA 92261

26. Theme Party Sing-Alongs: Lively sing-along tapes and matching song sheets for dozens of theme parties, as featured in this book, or custom-designed.
Address: Sing-Alongs; 47892 Oasis Court; Palm Desert, CA 92260

Unique and Innovative Products

27. Brainstorms Catalog: Wild and wacky items for gifts, prizes, favors, or props.
Phone: (800) 621-7500

28. Faux Rock and Granite Spray: Products to help you turn everyday recyclables into "concrete creations"—when you need to revert back to the stone age in your party planning. They're available at your local craft store. For your nearest dealer, call the numbers below:
Phone: (800) 842-4196 (Plaid Enterprises)
       (800) 797-3332 (Krylon)

29. First Impressions: Unusual Mailing Containers, Tubes, Envelopes: A large selection of offbeat mailing concepts.
Phone: (612) 595-8078 Fax: (612) 595-8615

30. Flax Art & Design Catalog: Hard-to-find and one-of-a-kind items that are ideal for gifts, prizes, awards, or favors.
Phone: (800) 343-3529

31. Flo-Fountain Centerpiece: A nifty item that will add excitement and glamour to your special events—to be placed on a buffet table or on your dining tables. A three-tier structure made of clear crystal-like plastic, this centerpiece contains a water reservoir to prolong the life of fresh flowers. It runs on batteries and can be used anywhere. A good investment, for yourself or your party pool. This company also has a rotating base for interesting decoration effects.
Phone: (800) 400-0047

32. Greetings from the President: A special, official, presidential greeting for a baby's birth, a wedding, a fiftieth-and-over anniversary, and a hundredth birthday. Allow four weeks for each request.
Address: The White House, Greetings Office, Room 39, 1600 Pennsylvania Avenue NW, Washington, D.C. 20500-1600

33. Karaoke Express: Professional-quality equipment at personal-use prices. Includes a variety of songs on disc. Purchase one for your party pool or organization.
Phone: (612) 879-4592

34. Magic Mounts: The perfect way to hang posters, signs, photos, decorations, lights, balloons, or any other light items, on walls, ceilings, or any delicate surface—without leaving a mark or stain. The special self-adhesive material can be removed and repositioned without fuss or muss. Many special-event venues will not allow hanging signs or decorations of any kind on the premises. These clever hangers will solve that problem.
Phone: (800) 332-0050

35. Panic Button by Memory Makers: Cute little gimmick idea—a red, computer-keyboard key labeled "Panic Button" that can easily be attached to any keyboard. Ideal for favors or promotional giveaways.
Phone: (360) 734-9506
e-mail: Silvanac@MSN.com

36. Party Holdems by Funzone: Products designed to relieve party guests of the hassle of balancing food, drinks, and personal items while trying to eat and socialize at the same time. These trays come in brightly colored craftboard, clear plastic, and dishwasher-safe plastic. They are a definite must for the party pool.
Phone: (714) 444-4FUN (ask for Debbie)

37. Think Big: Huge replicas of everyday items for props, clever awards, or displays.
Phone: (800) 487-4244

38. Votive candle holder with a checkered border trim: Can be found in Stump's Catalog.
Phone: (800) 22-PARTY

Planning Guides and Reference Materials

Before you invest any money, check out these books at your library. Then buy those you want to have in your permanent party-planning library. Cut expenses by creating a party/event planning library to be shared by your coworkers, as well as members of a homeowners', church, or school association.

39. *The Address Book: How to Reach Anyone Who Is Anyone,* by Michael Levine: Includes celebrities from the fields of entertainment, sports, business, or literary accomplishment. Add famous persons to your guest list, or request letters of congratulations and signed photos from your guest-of-honor's hero or idol. Published by Perigee Books.

40. *Are You Over the Hill?,* by Bill Dodds: The perfect gag gift jam-packed with fun ways to remind friends that their better years may be behind them. Published by Meadowbrook Press.

41. *The Best Baby Shower Book,* by Courtney Cooke: A contemporary guide packed with planning tips, decorating ideas, recipes, and activities. Published by Meadowbrook Press.

42. *The Best Party Book,* by Penny Warner: Creative ideas for seasonal parties and family events—everything you need to turn your parties into memorable celebrations. Published by Meadowbrook Press.

43. *The Best Wedding Shower Book,* by Courtney Cooke: Helpful planning tips, creative decorating ideas, tasty recipes, and fun activities. Published by Meadowbrook Press.

44. *Celebrate Today!,* by John Kremer: 4,000 reasons to celebrate, or to take a day off work. Holidays for every day of the year to brighten and enlighten your spontaneous celebrations. In *Celebration Creations Catalog* (see following listing); $12.95.

45. *Celebration Creations Catalog,* by Patty Sachs: Books, reports, software, and other products to inspire and assist you in planning successful and memorable special occasions and events.
Send $3 (refunded on order) to: Catalog, Dept. PP, 73-729 Manzanita Court, Palm Desert, CA 92260.

46. *The Envelope Mill,* by Haila Harvey: Step-by-step instruction kit for creating envelopes from distinctive papers and fabrics, to coordinate with your special theme. Includes templates in three sizes. In *Celebration Creations Catalog* (see above listing); $16.95.

47. *Every Day is Earth Day,* by Kathy Ross: Great projects for kids, to help teach the value and worth of honoring the earth, on this day and all others. In *Celebration Creations Catalog* (see above listing); $5.95.

48. *The Everything Bartender's Book,* by Jane Parker Resnik. Published by Adams Publishing.

49. *Family Reunions & Clan Gatherings,* by Shari Fiock: Start-to-finish tool for organizing reunions, centennials, or anniversaries. Sample forms, strategies, publicity tips, and search techniques. In *Celebration Creations Catalog* (see above listing); $12.95.

50. *52 Totally Unique Theme Parties,* by Patty Sachs: 52 miniplans that provide all the details necessary to create an offbeat theme party. In *Celebration Creations Catalog* (see above listing); $5.95.

51. *Gift Wrapping, Creative Ideas from Japan,* by Kunio Ekiguchi: Explanations and directions for gift-wrapping traditions of the Orient. Exquisite and intricate ways to create a gift of the wrapping itself. Published by Harper & Row Publishers; $19.95.

52. *The Great Song Thesaurus,* by Dick and Harriet Jacobs. A collection of songs you can use for any party, such as Victorian. Published by Writer's Digest Books.

53. *Guinness Book of Records:* If you plan an event that promises to be a record-breaker, contact the "Book" for how-to information.
Address: Facts on File, Inc., 460 Park Avenue South, New York, NY 10016

54. *Happy Birthday, Grandma Moses, Activities for Special Days throughout the Year,* by Clare Bonfanti Braham and Maria Bonfanti Esche: Almost 300 pages of innovative, how-to projects for traditional special occasions, as well as for dozens of less-celebrated events, such as Helen Keller's Birthday, World Health Day, and P.T.

Barnum's Birthday. A treasure chest of fun for the whole family. In *Celebration Creations Catalog* (see above listing); $14.95.

55. Party books for kids, by Penny Warner. Published by Meadowbrook Press. For more ideas on cooking for kids' parties and keeping the kids occupied during the festivities, the following books are great:
> *Kids' Holiday Fun*
> *Kids' Party Cookbook*
> *Kids' Party Games and Activities*

56. Kwanzaa books—for more information on the customs, traditions, cooking, and crafts, the following will be helpful:

The African American Celebration of Kwanzaa, by Maulana Karenga. Published by University of Sankor Press.

Crafts for Kwanzaa, by Kathy Ross. Published by Millbrook Publishing. In *Celebration Creations Catalog* (see above listing); $5.95.

Kwanzaa: An African-American Celebration of Culture & Cooking, by Eric V. Copage. Published by Quill Publishing.

Note: The following books by Kathy Ross are also available:
> *Crafts for Christmas*
> *Crafts for Thanksgiving*
> *Crafts for Halloween*
> *Crafts for Valentine's Day*

57. *Mall Treasure Hunt,* by Patty Sachs: Complete, step-by-step instructions for this wild-and-wacky romp through a mall, for groups of any size. The hunt takes about an hour, and can end at the mall, your home or office, or a banquet hall. It works beautifully for a luau or island-hopping theme.
Send check or money order for $6.50 (includes shipping) to: Treasure Hunt, P.O. Box 2200, Palm Desert, CA 92260.

58. Party game books, by Courtney Cooke. Published by Meadowbrook Press. Unique party-planer helpers that will help break the ice at and get the party off to a fast and funny start. Each book contains eight entertaining games and activities, and comes with tear-out duplicate game sheets for eight party guests.
> *The Best Bridal Shower Party Game Book*
> *The Best Couple's Shower Party Game Book*
> *The Best Baby Shower Party Game Book*
> *The Over-the-Hill Party Game Book*

59. *Reunions* (magazine)*:* A quarterly publication for reunion planners and attendees—addresses all details of organizing family, class, or association reunions. Subscribers receive a sixty-page workbook to use in the planning process.
Phone: (414) 263-4567

60. *Step-by-Step 50 Children's Party Cakes,* by Sue Maggs: Prize-winning cake designs for rave-getting cakes. Most designs are a bit of a challenge, but all are worth the effort. In *Celebration Creations Catalog* (see above listing); $9.98.

61. *Stress-Free Planning of Special Occasions,* by Patty Sachs: Quarterly newsletter filled with ideas, plans, and resources to help you plan any sort of event, from concept to cleanup. Special offer for readers of this book—$16 per year.
Send check to: Newsletter, P.O. Box 2200, Palm Desert, CA 92260

62. *Treasure and Scavenger Hunts: How to Plan, Create, and Give Them,* by Gordon Burgett: Spells it all out for you to create very individualized hunts for all age groups. In *Celebration Creations Catalog* (see above listing); $9.95.

63. *21st Century Eventologist,* by Adrienne Sioux Koopersmith: An incredibly creative collection of "holidates" to inspire you when you are looking for a good reason to plan a special event or party. Fund-raising events, promotions, or combination theme/personal occasion parties.
Write for information: ASK, 1437 West Rosemont, 1W, Chicago, IL 60660-1319

Associations and Event-Planning Services

When seeking a specialist in the party/event industry, you may want to contact the following agencies for the names of members in your area. Vendors with association membership are generally professional in their business and up-to-date in their equipment and expertise.

American Rental Association: (800) 334-2177
Association of Bridal Consultants: (203) 355-0464
ISES: International Special Events Society: (800) 688-4737
National Association of Balloon Artists: (904) 354-7271
National Association of Catering Executives: (708) 480-9080
National Association of Reunion Managers: (800) 654-2776
Society of American Florists: (703) 836-8700

Special Event, Wedding, and Party-Planning Web Sites

If you have any party/wedding planning questions or are looking for a resource, you can reach Patty Sachs at **partysachs@internetmci.com**. For more party links, try **http://www.angelfire.com/biz/CelebrationsPluS/index.html**. If you do not have Internet service in your home, use the public library computers, and print out whatever you find.
Surfing tips: For "case sensitive" addresses, use caps when shown. Some of these sites take a while to load, especially if your modem is less than 28800 (computer talk), so have some reading or handwork nearby. You may want to set up some exercise equipment next to the computer!

Information Sites

64. American Rental Association **http://www.ararental.org** Archived articles by experts, with fabulous party ideas and plans, plus the names of reliable rental companies near you.

65. Armory Square **http://www.armorysquare.com/guide** Dozens of articles about holidays, parties, and ethnic and traditional events.

66. Ask the Rabbi **http://virtual.co.il** Advice and guidance in planning Jewish events.

67. Balloon and Party Decorations **http://www.fooledya.com** Great tips designed for professionals.

68. Baskin Robbins **http://baskinrobbins.com** "Favorite" ideas for kid and adult parties. A fun site with lots of surprises.

69. Catering **http://www.autonomy.com** Catering resources, planning ideas, and links to other sites to party/event hosts.

70. Dawn Marie Designs **http://www.bombshells.com** A delightful site that displays information on glamour queens (for movie themes) and tells you where to find Victorian/vintage clothing and props. Be sure to click on *Elsie's Closet*.

71. Drink Ideas **http://webcouver.com/drinks** Learn to recreate potent potables with micrometer-level precision.

72. The 80s Server **http://www.80s.com/entrance.html** Loaded with trivia, music, and movie facts for your theme party games.

73. Family Advice **http://www.ktca.org/donnasdays** Donna Erickson, family activity expert, offers how-to information for adult/kid projects for party preparation pr actual party fun.

74. Home Entertainment **http://www.homearts.com** The best of *Redbook, Good Housekeeping, Country Living,* and more: A dandy site for home and family entertaining, especially holidays.

75. International Special Events Society **http://www2.ises.com** Provides access to special-event professionals, should you need professional help.

76. Michaels Stores **http://www.michaels.com** Crafty instructions for your celebrations of gifts.

77. Recipe Encyclopedia **http://www.epicurious.com**. Great for all kinds of food-related information.

78. Sixties Stuff **http://artitude.com** Tie-dyed clothing or lava lamps at this site.

79. *Smart Wine Magazine* **http://smartwine.com** The latest wine news and information.

80. Songs **http://archive.uwp.edu/pub/music/lyrics** The Lyric Page lists the words to thousands of songs (by artist and by title).

81. TV Bytes **http://www.parkhere.com/tvbytes** Includes theme songs from TV shows and commercials—and it keeps growing!

82. Wedding Links Galore **http://members.aol.com/weddlinks** The most complete collection of links to wedding-planning information sites.

Product Sites

83. Amazon Books **http://www.amazon.com** Thousands of titles on every subject, for reference, gifts, and prizes.

84. Crafts **http://www.craftmall.com** A wealth of craft supplies and products.

85. Party Planning **http://www.chipsbooks.com** C.H.I.P.S. books: advanced information on catering, floral arrangements, weddings, and so on.

86. Party Stuff **http://www.mallpark.com/party** Hundreds of party-related products and providers.

87. Puzzles **http://www.personalpuzzles.com** Customized crossword puzzles—make fun party favors.

Searching for Something?

88. http://www.yahoo.com Go to the site, type in your key words, such as "party planning," "bar/bat mitzvah," or "reunions," and make a search on one of the many services, such as Excite, Lycos, AltaVista, Infoseek, and so on. You'll also find hundreds of articles and references on such subjects as flower arranging, trivia, family fun, song lists, and all conceivable holidays.

89. http://www.infospace.com Try this site if you are planning a reunion and want to search for attendees. You will even find maps for precise locating.

90. Internet Yellow Pages Offers hundreds of sites that will enlighten you with recipes, how-to instructions, magazine articles, and much, much more.

Occasion	Atlanta, 70	Hawaii/Luau, 71	New York, New York, 73	Ozark Mountains, 74	Southwest, 75	West, 76	Britain/Pub, 77	Carribean, 78	Germany/Oktoberfest, 79	Greece, 80	Italy, 81	Japan, 82	Switzerland, 83	International Food Fest, 84	Casino/Gambling, 85	Circus, Circus, 86	Comedy, 87	Cruise Ship/Nautical, 88	Fair, County or State, 89	Farm Life, 90
Birthdays																				
First		•				•										•	•		•	•
Kid's		•				•								•		•	•		•	•
Bar/Bat Mitzvah																•	•	•		
Quinceanera																				
Teens		•		•	•	•	•	•	•	•	•	•	•	•	•	•			•	•
Twenty-First		•		•	•	•	•	•	•	•	•	•	•		•	•			•	
Thirtieth	•	•		•	•	•	•	•	•	•	•	•	•		•	•	•		•	•
Fortieth	•	•		•	•	•	•	•	•	•	•	•	•		•	•	•		•	•
Fiftieth	•	•		•	•	•	•	•	•	•	•	•	•		•	•	•		•	•
Sixtieth	•	•		•	•	•	•	•		•	•	•	•		•	•	•		•	•
Seventy-Fifth	•	•		•	•	•	•	•	•	•	•	•	•		•	•	•		•	•
Hundredth	•	•			•	•								•						
Wedding Occasions																				
Engagement/Rehearsal		•			•	•	•	•	•	•					•				•	
Shower		•			•	•			•					•	•	•			•	•
Couple's Shower		•	•		•	•	•							•	•	•				
Bachelor/Bachelorette															•	•				
Reception	•	•	•		•	•		•	•	•	•		•					•	•	•
Gift Opening																				
Anniversaries																				
First		•			•	•		•						•				•		•
Tenth		•	•	•	•	•	•	•	•	•	•	•	•		•	•	•	•	•	•
Twenty-Fifth		•	•	•	•	•	•		•	•	•	•	•		•	•	•		•	
Fiftieth	•	•	•	•	•	•	•	•	•	•	•	•	•		•					
New Baby																				
Shower		•			•	•										•	•			
Couple's Shower		•	•		•	•								•		•	•			
Graduations																				
High School		•	•	•	•			•									•		•	
College		•	•	•	•	•									•					
Life's Changes																				
Going Away/Moving	•	•	•	•		•									•				•	•
New Home																				•
Bon Voyage/Vacation		•	•		•	•		•	•	•	•	•	•		•				•	
Retirement		•				•									•					
Memorial Services																				
Reunions																				
Family		•			•	•									•				•	
Class		•			•	•									•	•			•	
Neighborhood/Block		•	•	•		•								•	•	•	•		•	•

Birthdays / Occasions Theme Index

Occasion	Fortune Telling, 91	Karaoke/Star Search, 92	Kindergarten, 93	Magic, 94	Mystery, 95	Over-the-Hill, 96	Pajama, 97	Starry Summer's Night, 98	Surfin' USA, 99	Tacky/Tasteless, 100	This is Your Life, 101	Prehistoric/Flintstones, 102	Toga, 103	Medieval, 104	Victorian, 105	Roaring Twenties, 106	Forties, 107	Fifties, 108	Sixties, 109	Seventies, 110	Wartime/M.A.S.H., 111	Futuristics Fantasies, 112
Birthdays																						
First			●	●				●														
Kid's	●	●	●	●	●		●		●			●										●
Bar/Bat Mitzvah	●	●		●	●				●		●											●
Quinceanera																						
Teens	●	●														●	●	●	●	●	●	●
Twenty-First	●	●		●		●	●	●	●	●	●		●	●		●	●	●	●	●	●	●
Thirtieth	●	●		●	●	●	●	●	●	●	●	●				●	●	●	●	●	●	●
Fortieth	●	●	●	●	●	●	●	●	●	●	●				●	●	●	●	●	●	●	●
Fiftieth	●	●	●	●	●	●	●	●	●	●	●	●	●	●	●	●	●	●	●	●	●	●
Sixtieth	●	●	●	●	●	●	●	●	●	●	●	●				●	●	●	●	●	●	●
Seventy-Fifth	●	●	●	●	●	●	●	●	●		●					●	●	●	●	●	●	●
Hundredth				●				●			●			●	●	●						
Wedding Occasions																						
Engagement/Rehearsal	●	●		●				●	●	●												●
Shower	●	●		●				●	●	●	●											
Couple's Shower	●	●		●			●	●	●	●												
Bachelor/Bachelorette	●			●				●	●	●										●	●	●
Reception	●			●				●					●	●	●	●	●	●	●	●		
Gift Opening																						
Anniversaries																						
First				●			●	●	●	●												
Tenth	●	●		●	●		●	●	●	●									●	●	●	●
Twenty-Fifth	●	●		●	●			●		●						●	●	●	●	●	●	●
Fiftieth	●			●				●			●					●	●	●	●	●	●	●
New Baby																						
Shower	●	●	●				●			●												
Couple's Shower		●	●	●	●		●		●	●		●										●
Graduations																						
High School	●	●	●	●	●				●	●	●	●							●	●	●	●
College	●	●	●	●	●		●		●	●	●	●	●						●	●	●	●
Life's Changes																						
Going Away/Moving										●	●											
New Home										●												
Bon Voyage/Vacation										●												
Retirement	●										●											
Memorial Services																						
Reunions																						
Family										●								●	●	●		●
Class											●						●	●	●	●	●	●
Neighborhood/Block	●	●	●	●	●				●	●								●	●	●		●

189

	Arts and Crafts	Board//Trivia Games	Books	Card Games	Collecting	Computers	Gardening	Gourmet Cooking	Hayride	Makeover/Minispa	Music	Night at the (Theater…)	Pets	Photography	Tools/Workshop	Travel	Bowling	Golf/Tennis	Health and Fitness	Hunting/Fishing	Ice/Roller Skating
Birthdays																					
First	●	●	●						●		●		●	●							●
Kid's	●								●		●		●	●			●				●
Bar/Bat Mitzvah									●		●		●	●		●	●	●	●	●	●
Quinceanera											●										
Teens	●	●	●	●	●	●				●	●	●	●	●	●	●			●	●	●
Twenty-First		●		●		●			●	●	●			●			●	●		●	●
Thirtieth		●	●	●	●	●	●	●	●		●		●	●		●					
Fortieth	●	●	●	●	●	●	●	●	●		●	●	●	●	●	●	●	●	●	●	●
Fiftieth	●	●	●	●	●	●	●	●	●		●	●	●	●	●	●	●	●	●	●	●
Sixtieth	●	●	●	●	●	●	●		●		●		●	●		●		●		●	●
Seventy-Fifth	●	●	●	●	●	●					●		●			●			●		
Hundredth	●	●	●				●	●			●					●					
Wedding Occasions																					
Engagement/Rehearsal				●				●	●		●			●		●					
Shower	●	●	●	●	●	●	●	●			●			●		●	●	●	●		●
Couple's Shower	●	●	●	●	●	●	●	●			●		●	●	●	●	●	●	●	●	●
Bachelor/Bachelorette											●						●	●	●		●
Reception		●						●			●					●					
Gift Opening																					
Anniversaries																					
First		●		●		●		●	●					●			●	●	●		●
Tenth	●	●	●	●		●		●	●					●		●	●	●	●	●	●
Twenty-Fifth	●	●	●	●		●	●	●	●		●					●		●			
Fiftieth	●	●	●	●		●		●			●					●					
New Baby																					
Shower	●		●		●		●	●	●	●	●		●	●		●				●	
Couple's Shower		●			●			●	●		●			●			●		●		
Graduations																					
High School		●				●			●		●			●			●	●	●		
College		●		●		●			●		●		●	●		●	●	●	●	●	●
Life's Changes																					
Going Away/Moving							●	●								●					
New Home	●						●	●							●						
Bon Voyage/Vacation														●		●					
Retirement	●	●	●	●	●	●	●	●	●		●	●	●	●	●	●	●	●	●	●	●
Memorial Services																					
Reunions																					
Family									●		●			●		●					
Class											●										
Neighborhood/Block									●		●								●	●	

190

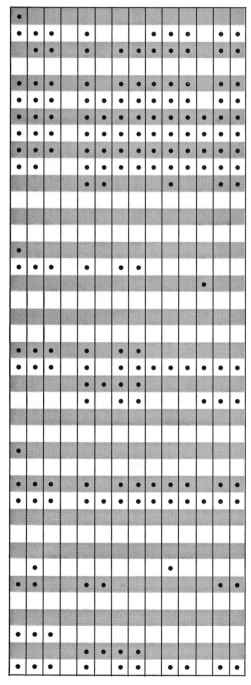

Birthdays
First
Kid's
Bar/Bat Mitzvah
Quinceanera
Teens
Twenty-First
Thirtieth
Fortieth
Fiftieth
Sixtieth
Seventy-Fifth
Hundredth
Wedding Occasions
Engagement/Rehearsal
Shower
Couple's Shower
Bachelor/Bachelorette
Reception
Gift Opening
Anniversaries
First
Tenth
Twenty-Fifth
Fiftieth
New Baby
Shower
Couple's Shower
Graduations
High School
College
Life's Changes
Going Away/Moving
New Home
Bon Voyage/Vacation
Retirement
Memorial Services
Reunions
Family
Class
Neighborhood/Block

Holidays	Far and Wide: USA						Far and Wide: World								Popular Themes					
	Atlanta, 70	Hawaii/Luau, 71	New York, New York, 73	Ozark Mountains, 74	Southwest, 75	West, 76	Britain/Pub, 77	Carribean, 78	Germany/Oktoberfest, 79	Greece, 80	Italy, 81	Japan, 82	Switzerland, 83	International Food Fest, 84	Casino/Gambling, 85	Circus, Circus, 86	Comedy, 87	Cruise Ship/Nautical, 88	Fair, County or State, 89	Farm Life, 90
New Year's Day		•			•	•								•						
M. Luther King, Jr. Day																				
Chinese New Year																				
Valentine's Day		•											•	•	•					
Mardi Gras															•					
President's Day															•					
Leap Year		•		•		•								•	•		•			
St. Patrick's Day																				
Easter		•			•	•	•							•					•	•
April Fool's Day		•			•	•	•							•		•	•			
Earth Day																				•
Cinco de Mayo																				
Mother's Day	•	•	•		•	•	•							•					•	•
Memorial/Veterans Day			•		•	•								•					•	•
Father's Day		•	•		•	•	•							•					•	•
Fourth of July		•			•	•								•					•	•
Bastille Day														•					•	•
Labor Day		•			•	•								•				•	•	•
Columbus Day													•					•		
Halloween	•	•	•	•	•	•	•	•	•	•	•	•	•	•	•	•	•	•	•	•
Thanksgiving														•					•	•
Hanukkah																				
Christmas		•			•	•								•						
Kwanzaa																				
New Year's Eve	•	•	•	•	•	•								•		•		•	•	•
Once in a Blue Moon																				